I0596888

AZURE: A JOURNAL OF LITERARY THOUGHT

a project of

Lazuli Literary Group

AZURE: A JOURNAL OF LITERARY THOUGHT
Volume One

Edited by
Sakina B. Fakhri & Diana McClure

with

Illustrations by
Evgenia Barsheva

LAZULI LITERARY GROUP
New York
2017

Lazuli Literary Group is a platform for the cultivation and advocacy of the imaginative faculty through a small press, contests, and an online/print literary journal. At a time when "facts" are so readily available through technological means, it is no longer necessary to invent a solution when you can "search" for one. In this context, the ability to imagine as a form of agency becomes paramount. We believe the value of creative writing and narrative fiction as tools to engage with social opinions, histories, and moral codes is vital to personal, political, and social evolution. On the level of craft, we advocate creative writing's ability to reveal interiority and its ability to transform, heal, and act as a catalyst for the full self-actualization of individuals and society. Aesthetically, we love work that is explicitly demanding of the reader linguistically, intellectually, and emotionally.

Published by Lazuli Literary Group | New York

www.LazuliLiteraryGroup.com

ISBN/SKU: 9780999424308
ISBN Complete: 978-0-9994243-0-8

Interior & Cover Illustrations: Evgenia Barsheva

Cover Design: Anders Jones

LAZULI LITERARY GROUP

home of *Otherworld Realism.*

otherworld realism

[**uh*th*** -er-**wurld**] [**ree**-*uh*-liz-*uh* m]

noun

1. a style of literature devoted to intellectual and imaginative pursuits that point towards a potential, evolved reality.
2. art and literature that evokes the space before clarity in which one must navigate the logic of intuition and instinct, alongside the duplicity of fact.
3. a genre illuminating a psychic space of process; a space of ambiguity, silence, and internal struggle.
4. the pre-dawn.

Word Origin

2017; coined by Lazuli Literary Group; first appearing in *AZURE: A Journal of Literary Thought, Volume One.*

TABLE OF CONTENTS

SUSURROS DE RECURRENCIA

by Franco Strong

She dreamed an endless, labyrinthine dream where shadows stretched over the abyss, where vivid colors sank into her skin, where the memories of the entire world were contained in a single drop of water that trickled down to the bottom of a forgotten riverbed. She dreamed because the liquid images were all she had left, all she could grasp with any certainty. Corrosive, dry years—along with too many days peering at the sun with her blue eyes—left her blind. Her vision had disappeared in gradual phases, like the moon, until the sliver of light finally faded and never returned. Muscles followed soon after, evaporated and useless in the perpetual drought of old age.

Yet the immobile darkness had its own landscape, its own dense valleys and open vistas for Quetzali to navigate. And in these unlocking, shifting, intertwining spaces her dreams were much more than simple reveries, they were her memories, pieces, fragments of a life that continued in a realm devoid of time and space.

She dreamed and remembered the days of spices, herbs, and roots, her young yet calloused hands pulling treasures from the desert soil and turning them into potions, remedies, and medicines. Those were days before the incursion of the intruders, the Spaniards, marched upon the land with skin white like cream and destroyed ancient cities only to rebuild atop the ruins.

In her life before the darkness she had been a healer, a woman of earthly medicines. The desert plains had whispered their secrets to her long ago and they still echoed faintly within the caverns of her dreams.

The liquid images of her mind began to solidify, she felt the sun against her skin, the granule scent of the plains filled her nose, she saw the receding horizon once again, her memories came alive…

Quetzali arrived at the entrance to a hut made of dried mud-bricks, her young hands armed with the ancient secrets of the earth. Her medicines were the last line of defense, the last barrier against the encroaching hands of death which consistently swept in like the western winds.

A man greeted and welcomed her in. He glanced over her with eyes that seemed like two shallow trenches dug up but quickly forgotten. The man wasn't too old but his joints and neck moved slowly and deliberately as though every split second he mentally measured out his movements. The adobe walls were cracked and splintering, clay pots were strewn across the ground, some broken, others half-filled with rotting liquid and food.

"I don't leave her side," the man said and then added, "I'm sorry. I don't see much of the sun. Your hair, it's so bright."

Even though Quetzali already knew the answers she still asked: how long has she been sick? How often did she eat? Was their blood in her vomit? When was the last time she spoke? Are the blisters on her skin peeling off yet? When was the

last time a Spaniard had been to their home?

After the man answered all the questions Quetzali asked one more, "And your children?"

"They are gone now," he answered. "Their mother lasted the longest. But even she hasn't opened her eyes in days."

The man led her to a small room, windowless, dark, a twin to the man's hollowed eyes. The man's life-partner, his spouse, lay huddled on a mat with a woven blanket pulled up to her chin. Quetzali knelt down and felt the sick woman's burning face. She told the man to go fetch some fresh water and food if he had any, and then to leave her alone so she could work upon the sick woman.

The heavy, monolithic air tasted of sickness and made the scar above Quetzali's brow line ache a bit. She lifted the blanket to examine the dying woman. Her body was covered in leaking sores with blotches of skin that resembled creatures only found in nightmares. Nothing could be done for this sickly woman, she was a breathing corpse, a human-sized piece of mucus ready to be dried out and then claimed by the desert sands just beyond the adobe walls. So many had already been taken, young, old, woman, man, child, the coughing-storm passed through the village with a blistering indifference, and it returned every year, hungrier than before. Quetzali had been spared, and sometimes she thought the plague had chosen her to be its eyes, to see and watch and remember all those who died in its grip. This sickly woman would be yet another, the herbs and medicine could do nothing except maybe offer a few moments of comfort before another life slipped away.

Quetzali's hands worked some of the remedies onto the woman's boiling and blistered skin. The reed mat which the sickly woman lay upon was covered in thick, coagulating human liquids. Quetzali started to clean the unconscious body when the man, the sickly woman's life-partner, reentered the room with a clay pot filled with water and a few pieces of dried meat in his hands.

"This was all I could find," he said.

Quetzali nodded then said she need to work here, alone.

"Can you help her?" he asked.

"With the blessings of the gods, maybe," she said. "Take this blanket, wash it."

The man gave one more pleading glance with his cavernous eyes before leaving again.

Using only the water of the clay pot, Quetzali washed the sickly woman's mouth, cheeks, and hair. A spectral echo of life returned to the dying face, but that was all. Her breath remained shallow, like ripples on a quiet lake. Quetzali patted more ointments, nectars, and pastes of dried leaves onto the swollen blisters. The woman let out a few unconscious moans, pure animalistic reflexes. The soul had already left the body, escaped though cracked lips and muffled breaths, and now it was wandering through the abyss, a lost murmur in the desert night.

Quetzali worked the dried meat between her teeth and spat it back into her hands before mixing it with a few roots she pulled from her leather pouch. Then she massaged the mixture into the sickly woman's mouth and made her swallow with a gulp of warm water.

"Rest," she whispered, "Let your soul find its way now."

After a short time the woman's breaths began to diminish like those puddles of rain left behind after a storm. Quetzali struck two pieces of cheyrt together and ignited a small pile of sage. The scent and glimmer of light was for the lost souls, to help them find their way. Quetzali had done this too many times, ushered too many through the valleys of nothingness. She wondered if they'd be waiting for her when she died, a small army of souls smelling of burnt sage and eyes casting distant reflections of smoldering embers.

The soft glow died out and the room reverted back to obscurity as the earthy scent siphoned into the cracks of the walls. Silence arose and Quetzali knew that the woman had inhaled her last breath some time ago, that another bleak finality had arrived. A consuming fatigue descended upon Quetzali's bones, the same one that followed all the other nameless faces, but Quetzali clasped onto the small notion that the earth's immortal sin—suffering—had somehow been reduced, lessened. She uttered prayers over the lifeless body and reminded herself that her work was good, her hands were clean, that they would remain clean. Against the weight of the earth's cruel providence her own trespasses meant nothing, her hands were only there to gather whatever fragments remained, delicate and invisible.

A shuffle of approaching footsteps and muffled voices broke through the dense silence of the room. The man entered, followed by another man, taller, whose broad shoulders reminded Quetzali of tree trunks and eyes reminiscent of the leafless trees of a cold winter.

His low voice echoed between the small walls, "Get her away. She's done nothing here, nothing good flows from her."

The spousal husband dropped to his knees and cradled the limp body of the sickly woman. "She's dead. She's gone," he said and repeated it once more to himself.

Quetzali's eyes scanned the room "Who is this man? Why have you brought him here?" she asked. "The work isn't done, I must finish."

The first man, the spouse, didn't reply to Quetzali's words, only cursing himself, the walls, this sickness, before muttering, "You've killed her. You came here to kill her, like the others."

"Yes," the tall man said, "She's killed them all. None make it alive."

Quetzali stood and faced the tall stranger and held his gaze. "You speak of things you do not know."

The tall man said nothing, only swayed slightly as though caught in a breeze. The other man, the husband, shook the limp, sickly body, delicately, quietly.

"Do I know you, stranger? Have I wronged you? You come with venomous words," Quetzali said.

The husband, who was still clutching the lifeless hairs of his wife, spoke, "He found me. He came to me and warned me about you, about this. You leave a trail of death."

The tall man moved closer and added, "How many have survived? How many men, women, children, have been taken?"

"Sickness is sickness, it has no preferences," she said. "Its frigid hands reach everywhere."

"No, it doesn't take you," the tall man said, "It doesn't take them, the invaders of our lands."

Caresses of distortion lurched within Quetzali's mind. A warm sensation gathered, then slipped and stretched over her brow line. Her fingertips reached up to the scar beginning to tear open, the wound beginning to leak blood.

The tall man approached, looming over, "Blue eyes, from you mother or father? Or do you even remember where your blood comes from?"

Quetzali cursed and lunged at the tall man but he easily grasped both of her wrists and held. The herbs and potions fell from Quetzali and scattered across the dirt ground.

The tall man spoke as though his tongue was coated in a thick poison and spat out the heavy words, "Mother of the plague."

The vapors of the man's words lingered in her nostrils, but then the memory evaporated, her previous life vanished, and Quetzali was plunged back into her withered and blind body. The opaque dreamscape surrounded her once again, the steady ache of old-age lurked in her joints. She dreamed of a blackness that morphed into the night sky, empty of stars, then one, two at first, and slowly more gathered, points of light rupturing through the veil of darkness, then each star began to drip with light, until the brightness overflowed and fell out of the sky, down to earth, like tears forming into an ocean, and Quetzali felt herself sinking, gasping for air, drowning on the churning chunks of white foam. Then, through the waves, she felt the comforting and familiar sensation of hands, calloused yet young, holding her body, grasping her fingers, caressing her hair, and for a moment everything became calm once again.

If he peered at her face long enough he sometimes saw the faint outline of the woman he had known in his childhood: blue eyes, skin carved by the sun, light-brown hair like the roots of the mesquite. His calloused hands caressed her gray hair, now brittle from a lifetime of soaking in sunlight. Her withered and blind body lay on one side, curled upon itself like a child. She opened her eyes—white with cataracts, two spheres of pure sunlight—then moaned, the sound reminiscent of a summer rainstorm over the barren plains. Her long fingers reached out and he held them, gently. Blood began to trickle from the scar cauterized upon her forehead.

"Grandmother, I'm here," he whispered in her ear, "Quetzali, it's your grandson, Surem. It's alright, rest now."

Her blind eyes lulled from one side across to the other, searching. The moans slowly subsided but her fragile grip remained upon Surem's fingers. Her lips moved, faintly, as though they were tracing over an echo and Surem leaned over, trying to make out the words of his grandmother, but he only felt the subtle, distilled warmth of dying breaths against his ears.

There was little time left for her. Days ago the Spanish holy-men had come to give her the final Christian blessing, but the old woman still fought for life, almost as though she were mocking them and their feeble Christ-Child. No one else had come to see her though, none of her own people, none of her own tribe. It seemed as though the entire village had forgotten her, a stain scrubbed from their collective memory. Soon she'd join Surem's parents in the wasteland of the forgotten. He possessed only a few corroded images of his mother and father, spectral images devoid of faces. Their deaths had come suddenly when he was only a small boy and the task of raising Surem had been left to this woman, his grandmother. Her austere, blue eyes had guided him through the lessons of becoming a man more so than any of those forced upon him by the Spaniard's schooling. She had knowledge of a time before the arrival of the crosses, whips, *caballos*, *iglesia*, and those thunder-sticks which can strike a man down in an instant, a time before the sweeping plague, a time before death. Even as she lay there inert, her blue eyes washed-out in white, he felt she still had more to teach him, that there were too many holes riddled throughout his mental landscape that only she could fill. If she had one more day with a clear mind and a voice that didn't crack like dead leaves. He dribbled a wet cloth upon his grandmother's peeling lips so the dead air wouldn't seize her throat.

Piled high against one corner of the adobe room were bones, hides, stones, each engraved with a tangle of symbols. Surem shuffled through them, examining, rearranging pieces, fitting one against the other. He recalled watching his grandmother as a young boy, her slender fingers scrambling over themselves to engrave the strange symbols, whether in the early morning light or the glow of the full moon, her lips silent, never releasing the secrets she so carefully etched out. Now, as she was dying and Surem spent countless days beside her, he studied those engravings, desperate to find a remedy, a cure, something to regain lost time, lost health, a way to decipher those secrets that died in her shadows. It had to be somewhere in there, in those shambles of symbols, in a language he couldn't fathom.

He had asked her once, as a child, what they were for, what those enigmatic symbols meant. She only replied that they were for her memories, for the ones that she could never recover because they lay buried beneath the dry land, memories of a past, memories of a future. She forbade him to look upon the engravings and told him it was best to forget, to never see what she had gazed upon.

Surem pulled out a few more bones alongside another rawhide and looked them over. Desert sand clung to each crevice of the engravings, as though the earth were already reclaiming something. He carefully laid out the pieces, trying to reassemble the complex web of connections, his busy hands pale, lost reflections of his grandmother's from years ago. The white cataracts of her eyes dripped with a veil of milky white. Surem's fingers worked to peel back the layers of gravel accumulated atop the years, to renew these echoes, to listen to the shadows of the desert—the ever-absent sea—whisper its secrets once again.

The tremors grow in violence until you are engulfed completely, like a great chasm has suddenly opened up to swallow you, a dead region between spaces. Then everything is dark and silent, except for the slight vibrations behind your ears. You cry out, just to drive away the silence, and you hear your own voice, tiny, frail, ready to crumble like the ash of a fire. The voice is that of a child, you, this lost child. It takes a moment for your mind to register that yes, this voice is your own, that you are nothing more than a slight youth. You try to move your arms, legs, torso, anything, but a cold pressure suffocates you, holds you down, renders your attempts less than useless. Your eyes gather nothing, only an infinitely long shadow that swallows the moments, a shadow that seems hungry to devour time itself. Your lungs cough up the vaguely familiar taste of earth and dust. You cry out once more, but this time to fill the void that has burrowed into your mind, into your thoughts. You have no memories, no recollections of a time before the darkness. A burning sensation creeps across your head and cheek. Tears soon follow, and you feel them fall from your face, claimed by the echoing nothingness that claims you. They were your tears, tears without memories and therefore tears like those of a newborn, plunged into the sublime terror of life, severed and separated from your own past.

Quetzali knew that she was dying, that she couldn't lay claim to her life much longer. Her soul was leaving her body through the pores of her ragged skin. She wandered through the barren dreamscape, a desert of forgotten time, as clouds gathered above. The wind blew stronger, rain fell to the ground. The storm coalesced into the images of another life, another memory of her youth…

She silently waited for nightfall and the cover of moonlight. Soon they'd arrive, all of them, nocturnal creatures of the night, with paws and snouts ready to unearth the sins buried beneath the dirt. She foresaw it, written there and inscribed in the symbols she had etched out in the bones and rawhides she kept, whispered to her by forgotten voices in the winds.

Her grandson, Surem, lay submerged in sleep, his adolescent body of skinny limbs reminded her of leafless tree branches. They were more than blood-relatives, more than simply grandmother and grandson, their existences intertwined within the prismatic, still waters of time. She uttered a prayer on his behalf, asking the gods for protection for both her and her grandson, before leaving her pueblo.

She crossed through the domain of earth and stars as she had done countless times before, but her tired hands weren't carrying the usual medicines and remedies. Instead they clutched a spear and a small dagger made of wood, sharpened stones, tied together with dried roots. She ran farther away, out to the dead lands, where the soil was too dry for life, the place where the village buried their dead. The earth cracked and sighed beneath her feet as though it had been waiting for her. Mounds of soil stretched out in every direction, forming an outline of the subterranean labyrinth of dead souls that lay beneath. How many had she put there? How many had she led along the journey just before death? How many sins could the desert hide, stored away and buried, but never forgotten?

She stopped and listened. The exhaling winds carried yelps, howls, and animalistic laughter of the beasts gathering in the distance. The sounds grew louder, closer, a sea of paws shuffled through the ancient gravel, descending upon Quetzali. Her hands gripped the spear and dagger as she silently mouthed one last prayer.

They were watching her, she sensed them, circling, a writhing mass of fur, saliva, and teeth. Their collective howl turned into an unwavering drone before dying down once again. Then Quetzali heard their paws beginning to dig, scratching away the surface of those loose mounds of dirt which kept more than just the dead sealed within. Her eyes focused on a shadow in the darkness, one directly ahead, and she lowered the spear. Her arms jerked. The sharpened tip found its mark, plunging deep into fur and muscle, the fatal blow delivered followed by a yelp of pain and a string of soft whimpers. Her hands—almost possessed by another spirit—repeated the action again and again, the yelps of pain identical as three coyotes fell to Quetzali's feet. Warm blood trickled down the spear and gathered on Quetzali's fingertips.

An ocean of glimmering eyes and yellow fangs faced her, their hot breaths pressed upon the cool air of the night. The coyotes gnawed on the decayed flesh and bodies they dug up from the earth, their primal, ancient instincts subsumed by the night. The scent of saliva and death haunted her, a reminder of her failure and the bleak misery she had brought to these people, to this village. Soul after soul had been lost because of her, because of the blood which flowed through Quetzali's veins and kept her alive throughout the plague-ravaged years. These coyotes wanted to burrow into the past and remind her of the sins she carried, the burden of her existence, and the impossible atonement she craved every aching moment.

No, Quetzali wouldn't let these pack of

beasts have their way. Her spear pierced through flesh once more, then again, and again. A set of jagged teeth punctured and tore through her own skin. She grunted and lashed out with the stone dagger, driving it somewhere into the attacking animal's neck, its final breath spilled into warm liquid upon her knuckles. From out of the darkness more fangs pierced and tore at the flesh of her arms, shoulders, legs. More fatal blows unleashed from her hands but her attacks slowed, tired, the fatigue in her forearms turned her muscles to useless, dangling stones.

The blood of her wounds spilled out and mixed with that of the dying coyotes before the parched earth sucked down the warm bits of moisture, impervious of its origins, thirsty for more. The fangs became relentless, unforgiving, as though they were an extension of the night itself, thousands of razored teeth lined across the horizon, sewn together by squeals and howls, a monolithic maw that precedes the absolute void. Quetzali staggered though the piles of whimpering coyotes, her bleeding body surrendering to the onslaught, collapsing onto the mound of loose gravel, waiting for the desert to claim her.

Face-down, her lips tasting the particles of earth, Quetzali whispered another prayer, urging the words to reach the labyrinth of bodies below. Finally, she could give her wretched blood to all those lost souls, to the desert, and her sins would finally be finished.

A small, indistinct glow appeared somewhere in the distance, approaching, splicing open the night of jaws and fur. The coyotes howled in pain as the light grew stronger, brighter, closer. It reached Quetzali and she peered up and saw a silhouette with two eyes, human eyes, eyes that made her shiver because they were colder than a winter out in the open plains. She recognized them, they belonged to a man, tall, the man who knew exactly who she was.

The man waved a torch and his voice echoed, "Get up. These burial grounds are not your own."

Massive arms, the arms of a nocturnal giant, pulled Quetzali onto her feet. Her dry and bloodied hands still gripped the granite dagger, and in the smoky haze that enveloped her consciousness she lashed out, her hands still searching for flesh and fur.

The voice came through like an ancient command, "Stop fighting, stop struggling. It's useless."

Quetzali watched as the tall man used only the torch and his bare hands to beat down the advancing coyotes, grabbing coats of fur, throats, snouts, and heaving the animals to the ground, the reflection of the flame cast in the innumerable set of translucent, yellow eyes.

"We must defend them, these dead here, their memories. You have to help me," she cried out, her desperate fingertips reaching out past the light of the torch and into the darkness searching for more animals to slay, more blood to let flow into the parched earth.

"These are not your dead. Not your ancestors. Not your people," he said. His forearms continued to lash out at the wild, screeching animals. "It was you who brought misery and death. These coyotes only followed the scent, your blood, the wake you leave behind," the man shouted.

Quetzali's hands still prowled through the darkness, her blade slicing only the solid night-air. "I came to help, I foresaw it." Mocking howls of the coyotes descended against Quetzali's temples.

Palms—massive and unmoving—seized and held her, these hands and fingers which she intimately knew, their touch familiar. Her face met his in the epicenter of light and she peered at his eyes, two bottomless wells devoid of water.

"You don't know," she whispered to him, "You can't comprehend."

The torch-fire danced between the man's wrinkled lips. "They've whispered your secrets, they've revealed it to the land. The earth has already tasted your blood." Then he added, "You child of Christ. You Spaniard."

Those words burrowed themselves into Quetzali, into the scar that ran along her brow line, and the keloid skin seemed to unravel, and her blood, Quetzali's liquid sins, spilled onto the desert and the ground seemed only hungry for more.

Then the world seemed to be suspended, unmoving and placid. First the man disappeared, then the light, like disseminating ether. Then the coyotes followed too, their yellowed eyes extinguished. And then the mounds of earth crumbled, flattened, until nothing of the memory was left and Quetzali's body turned old and sour, and she returned to the nocturnal, barren lands of her dying dreamscape. She found herself in the middle of a dry lake bed. It was a starless night, the horizon missing as though it had lost the ancient battle with existence. Cracks riddled the ground and slowly they began to widen beneath her thin feet, growing larger. She tried to run and escape but the gaps only opened further, just ahead of her fleeing steps, until a great chasm swallowed her into a frigid, timeless, eternally black moment.

The two crossed lines loomed above Surem's head, sitting atop the Spaniard's *iglesia*. The wooden cross stood in defiance to that other god, the sun. The Spaniards had taught Surem that their *Jesuscristo* had risen from death after three days. But Surem thought that mattered little because the sun lived a daily death, plunging into the fiery evening-horizon, only to arise anew each morning.

The day had just begun as Surem descended the flight of stairs that led into the basement of the Spanish church. Other men followed, their faces like his, forlorn, deep-set creases, eyes which held invisible scars. Despite the perpetual shade the sun's slithering heat still reached the cramped corridors below.

With a minimal amount of words the men filed themselves into a loose line, the corridors scarcely larger than the men's shoulders, and began their routine of passing bundles of corn, beans, and squash, storing them into the farthest reaches of the cellular chambers, those regions with small traces of relief from the omnipotent sun.

Disembodied calls of, "Wait!...Pass!... Hold!..." issued from the dimmest corners. Surem worked with his hands leading him, brushing against leathered-skin and callouses heavier than stone. The work was grueling, oxygen seemed to slowly siphon out of the corridors as breaths grew heavy, leaving Surem to inhale the sour perspiration of others. But the work here was better than being out in the fields, toiling beneath the unforgiving sun, where men constantly collapsed out in the open, choking on the purified light as the Spaniards gazed with indifference atop their four-legged beasts. And in these catacombs there were whispers, glimpses and echoes of a time before.

The subterranean network of passageways had been built long before the arrival of the Christ-God. The Spanish had erected their own temple atop the ruins of the old, the ancient gods had lost the battle against the Holy Trinity and were driven into hiding below ground, lurking in all that was left of their once towering home: subterranean passageways winding through stone foundations. At times Surem felt he was passing through the ancient gods themselves, but their voices went unheard, their whispers softer than smoke and almost forgotten. Surem possessed other memories though, more than just his own, those inscribed within the engravings of his grandmother, future memories that seemed to direct him as though her hands were present and guiding him.

As the other men worked Surem slipped away and descended farther into the small network of corridors. He went searching for a hidden piece, one that his grandmother mentioned in passing, a stone that held the old and new worlds in place, a promise of new life amongst the ancient. He allowed himself to be guided by her aura, yet he thought of her back home, alone and withering away in a useless body. Her salvation could be found down here though, the fragments of a shattered existence could be reassembled. In his grandmother's engravings there were references to a clear stone, a sort of prismatic gap that contained all the memories of the world. This stone was the center-point, the epicenter, an exact middle that held everything together, right in the heart of the old temple. Through the convoluted mess of etchings and engravings that his grandmother had left behind, one message kept reappearing: a new life, a new salvation was to be found amongst the crumbled walls of the world, memories would regain a vivid existence, a return to a time and a place where sin and salvation meant nothing.

He stumbled through room after room with his hands groping across the darkness, at times stumbling over his own feet. The corridors seemed to open farther, bend, shift, unfold upon themselves, like a mute, slow dance of twisting walls. His fingers finally fell upon a set of stones stacked atop each other that formed a simple, unassuming arch. The stones were cold and his fingers blindly climbed upward until they reached the apex which was exactly even with Surem's eye-level, though he couldn't see it, only caress blindly. At the center of the apex lay a triangular stone, the one he had been searching for, the minuscule prism that contained the unforgotten memories, the stone that saw all and remembered all.

Surem pulled his hands back and his mind contemplated all the possibilities inherent within the triangular stone. He thought of his grandmother, of the words she'd never say, of the stories she'd never reveal, but they were here, contained only within this stone. He contemplated his own past and if it was also inscribed within those three points, running parallel to his grandmother's. Her life had always been shrouded in silence, unexamined, as was his own. Was he prepared to retrace those years that had passed so easily in silence? Maybe his grandmother never spoke of their past, joined and separated at times, because the keloid scars were better left closed than opened to bleed once again. For a moment he doubted his grandmother's engravings, the loose, convoluted shards that had no chronological order and only repeated the same notions in an infinite amount of series. No, her ghostly hands had guided him this far, led him to this place, this stone, there was no denying it now. Time wasn't ripe yet though. His fingers touched upon the center-stone once again. He needed them, the Spaniards, to be gathered above, witnesses to the new horizon that would accompany the crumbling of their wretched walls.

Surem left the black chamber and retraced his steps through the darkness, back towards the light of the sun, and joined the others just as their exhausting work came to an end. Every last bushel of harvested crop had been stored away and the men began the trek out from their temporary tombs. Topside, the sun had already fallen below the horizon but its heat still clung to the air as though the sun were still claiming what it was rightfully owed. A few of the Spanish holy-men handed out meager portions of dry cornmeal and Surem grabbed his small ration in silence.

Then a voice pierced the air and disturbed the comfort of the sun in freefall. Clouds of dust rose into the sky with more voices chasing, then surpassing, the upward flight. A Spaniard atop a four-legged-beast wrenched a worker from out of the crowd, a rope firmly set around the man's neck. Another Spaniard atop a beast proceeded to whip the bare back of the worker out in the open for all to see. The leather line traced out a curve through the evening air, and the separation between this world and a bleeding oblivion seemed to be concentrated on the very tip of the whip which split open naked flesh. The man cried out and his voice hung in the air a moment longer as though it were carrying the collective pain of those gathered, a pain that only doubled as the seasons washed away. A screech of the whip, then flesh torn open, again, again, again. Then, just as easily, it was over, the man was released, free to internalize the pain as the land and the sun returned to their implacable indifference. The Spaniards rolled up their ropes and spoke in that slithering tongue of theirs before riding off atop their massive beasts.

Surem watched as the injured man lay motionless and bleeding, his prostrate arms embracing the ground, his blood offered to the arid soil, as though he were willing himself to become a part of the earth, as though his only desire at that moment was to become just another memory buried within the earth.

Your mind is a dry lakebed, a starless night, devoid of orientation. You have forgotten everything. You only know with a fleeting certainty that you are young, trapped in darkness, helpless. You try to push through the fog that has entangled your thoughts, your mind, your being. The buzzing in your head grows like winged insects in the early stages of flight. All you can remember is the terrible noise, the severed sounds, the great tremor that has fostered you, that created you, that has endowed you with existence, your very life has arisen from that single pulsation, a nameless daughter of a nameless calamity.

You try to move your body but your frail limbs are still held down by a great, dense, black pressure. You feel the tears fall from your face, down into a quiet expanse, and that makes you shed more tears because those intimate, liquid pieces of you are falling to the wayside, lost and subsumed by that void.

Suddenly, over your own whimpering voice, you hear traces of echoes, slight vibrations, stirrings of life beyond. You scream, a primordial scream, and your vocal chords are slowly shredded as you push them to the upper and highest registers possible. Voices, human voices float through the black and you listen, but there are others also, ancient voices endowed with the rasp of the endless sands, joining together in a quick succession then dying off once again. Through it all you hear that other voice, a human voice, calling out, and you answer back. Then a pinpoint of light pierces through the darkness, flickering, trembling, like the first star amongst the heavens struggling for life.

Dreams escaped Quetzali for a long time and she experienced nothing except her own approaching death in complete blindness. Her memories, too, had taken leave of her and fled from her dying presence. The drought that is old age had arrived with its slithering, choking finality. What more was left for a blind, immobile old woman? She was ready for her body to be reclaimed by the desert winds, for her impure soul to join the wasteland of the forgotten, to face all those souls with embers of burning sage within their eyes. Yes, they would be there, all of them, she could hear their calls already. The voices joined together in unison, a rolling chorus, and they sang of sin and atonements long forgotten, of one last memory…

It was a time of innocence, a time of beginnings, a time when the name Quetzali meant nothing to her. She had another name once, a Castilian name, taken from the Virgin Mother, the name given to her at birth had been Maria-Valentina. Small, adolescent hands gripped the stem of a vanity mirror and she gazed upon the face of a child with round, reddened cheeks, a jawline and chin reaching out from a young neckline, brown hair with hints of infant-blond, and morning-blue eyes, the centerpieces of a child's face, a face she recognized as her own.

She was seated at a desk of mahogany-wood. Above, a small marble Christ presided over the young girl and the stifling heat of the small room. His stone body hung to the cross against the wall, His head downcast with a crystal and unwavering gaze. It was almost time to go see Him, the man who always watched and silently kept track of the world's sins. Those were the things that they taught her in Sunday school at the holy church, sin, atonement, impurity, salvation. They also taught her that she needed to look her best on the Day of the Lord, so Maria-Valentina softened her hair with a few more brush strokes then tied a blue ribbon atop her head. She peered up at the marbleized Christ, forever frozen in that moment of agony, His suffering a constant renewal, and she wondered if her appearance lessened His pain. At times she had to fight the urge to pull the suffering Christ down and whisper to Him that no one needed to die for her sins, that she couldn't stand the thought of anyone dying just for her to live. But her hands never reached out to Our Savior, *Jesuscristo*, and His presence remained on the wall as a simple reminder of all things.

A wispy voice called out to Maria-Valentina and then her mother appeared in the doorway. Lace hanging from a beige dress ruffled at her mother's feet. She spoke in a wet, Castilian tongue, "Are you ready, *Mija? Vamos.* We'll be late."

Her father waited outside beneath the unforgiving sun, sweating, his great brow line offering the only vestiges of shade to his blue eyes, eyes that he had passed down to Maria-Valentina like water trickling downstream. The three of them walked together—father, mother, daughter—along the dirt path, the earthen ground wheezing and exhaling small plumes of dust beside their feet. Her mother spoke, her Castilian lips complaining about this miserable town, about the incessant heat of the land, how dry it was, how only savages could make a life here, how she missed home, *España*, its roads paved in cobblestones, the churches around every corner, and those evening rains of Madrid. Her father only nodded his head in agreement, saving his words for a later time.

Maria-Valentina had never been to her parents' homeland. She was a child of here, born in this parched earth which they called the New World, *Nuevo España.* Though whenever Maria-Valentina looked out across the plains dotted with beige boulders and the lethargic mountains in the horizon, this land, its colors, its people, appeared more ancient than anything else. It was *España* with its castles, grand churches, endless roads and endless lights that seemed like a new world to Maria-Valentina's young imagination, a foreign land built atop a dream.

As they made their weekly pilgrimage to the House of God they greeted others like themselves, castaway Spaniards, Spaniards who answered the call of The Church to domesticate a savage continent, but they also passed those that had already learned how to forge a life in this merciless land. A few of the *indigenos* bowed slightly while others kept their gaze focused on the cloudless distance, their forlorn faces and nocturnal eyes a stark contrast to the open sky. Maria-Valentina felt her father's arm guide her closer to him like she was the only precious treasure to be found in the desert.

The *iglesia* of Our Lord lay on the other side of town and it slowly came into view along with its cross that stood looming over the rest of the town's dismal buildings. No man and no building was allowed to rival His Glory. A steady, monotonous echo rang out from the church bells, prompting the family to hasten their pace. But Maria-Valentina noticed that the sound had no effect upon the passive faces of the *indigenos*. Maybe they were only accustomed to the whispers inherent within the empty plains and their ears couldn't register the alien, metallic chimes. Maria-Valentina had heard those whispers herself on quiet nights, when *la luna* left a ripple as it passed through the liquid night sky. Sometimes those voices called out to her by name, a different name, one she couldn't comprehend but undoubtedly knew was hers. She never spoke to anyone about the desert voices outside her windows, especially her parents. She told herself that some secrets were better kept buried within.

Before passing beneath the arched doorway of the *iglesia* Maria-Valentina followed her parents' lead and crossed herself with holy-water and the bit of moisture felt nice against her warm head. The midday sun shined upon the stained-glass windows and Maria swore that the brilliant colors must have come straight from Heaven. Her mother sat them close to the front because it was better to be closer to God's word. Maria looked back to the mass of *indigenos* standing outside the doorway, a sea of eyes and torn rags barely covering naked bodies. Their blood was still impure, they hadn't been redeemed by blessings so they were barred from His grace and His body.

The Priest took his place at the head of his parish and a hushed quiet settled between the walls. He only uttered a few opening words before an almost ephemeral tremor crossed over the ground, a yawn from the earth. A collective gasp escaped the throats of those gathered. The tremor subsided for a moment, the Father attempted to speak once again, but the tremor returned, stronger this time. The quivering earth grew more intense, turning violent, and the walls of the *iglesia* creaked in distress. Precious metals, candles, prayer-books fell to the tiled floor in echoing succession. The Father tried to yell over the crowd, urging them to remain calm because they were in God's temple, but his voice was drowned out. Maria reached out and clasped her mother just as the crucified Christ fell to the floor. Scattered cries for help bounced through the air as people scrambled to escape. The trembling grew into a consuming roar, as though the earth was splitting open within its innermost depth to reveal the gaping, mauling void that lay at the center of all things. Maria's father grabbed her and her mother, but a writhing mass of desperate bodies separated them from the doors that led outside to the safe, open air. Cracks spread through the walls and shards of stained-glass rained down upon the trapped victims, slicing the worshippers below with a thousand miniscule slashes upon their skin, crystal prisms of red, green, blue, yellow, lodging themselves within soft flesh.

Maria's blue eyes watched as the *iglesia* collapsed and crumbled around her, great pieces dropping from the ceiling and smashing into the poor, ensnared souls below. And amidst the catastrophe a vague notion seized Maria, that she had dreamt this calamity before, in another life, in another name, that a chorus of forgotten voices had already sung these scenes to her, those voices she heard out in the desert on silent nights. Her young mind tried to reach out and give shape to that mental landscape she envisioned before—somewhere she heard her mother's cries, she saw her father's outstretched hands—but the roaring seized her soul, a chasm of echoing nothingness seemed to open its jagged jawline and consume Maria, replacing her collection of memories with a dripping, black saliva.

A petrified sorrow sank into Surem's hands then slowly crept into the rest of his body, like roots groping through arid soil. Three days have passed—he counted each painted-sky fall into the evenings—yet he hadn't moved. He remained focused on that body which lay before him, inert, still, devoid of life: the body of his grandmother Quetzali. In her last moments she exhaled simple, almost painless croons as though the eroding wind had already claimed her voice. Her opaque, crystalline eyes still lay open to the world, its sky, its horizons, its faces, a world she hadn't seen in years, a world she'd never see again.

He had left her body untouched after her last breath had fallen because there was no use, the vital spark of her soul had been lost to the wastelands of the remembered. It mattered little where her body lay, whether beneath a mound of earth or beneath the eviscerating sun, inevitably her flesh would be reclaimed and possessed once again by the desert sands. The raw, carrion stench reminded Surem that the process was already underway.

The trace amounts of moisture found in the morning air gave way to the stale, midday sun just outside the walls of the hut. Surem tried to recall time spent with his grandmother but the only vision that came to him was that of her blue eyes and the way in which they seemed to comprehend the world differently than all the others of their village. What had those blue gems seen? What memories lay behind which injected her world with something unseen by others? And when her eyes had become blinded and sun-streaked what world did she inhabit, a place of perpetual light or immobile shadows? Or maybe she lived in the boundaries of both, a convergence of harsh oblivion and somber tragedy, a collapsed perspective of existence and oblivion in equal measure.

Pieces of her still remained though, in those scattered engravings of bones, rawhides, and colored stones she left behind. Surem stood, his back and knees aching, to examine the intricate web of symbols once again. They were his undertaking, a reconstruction of his grandmother's work as she lay dying. He had deciphered bits and pieces, enough to understand their full significance, symbols which conveyed notions of a return, a time without sin, a closing of circles, the collapsing walls of the new gods. Others needed to witness what Surem already knew, what only he possessed, the knowledge of the forgotten time was to return today—he had seen it, there, repeated in the engravings—three days after his grandmother's death.

Outside the foreign, metallic ring of church bells echoed through the distance and announced the day of worship for the Spaniards. They resonated but the sounds seemed to morph over a great distance, change, take on another dimension, like a chorus of voices calling him. And those voices were almost familiar, like he heard them before, in another lifetime, voices that reminded him of childhood, but not his childhood, that of another's, someone he had known intimately well. They called to him, to be renewed, to be reclaimed, to be purified but never forgotten, whispers and voices. Surem uttered his own prayer before leaving his grandmother in the stale sunlight of the adobe room and walked outside, his first sunlight in days.

He made his way to the center of town and followed the dirt path towards the bells, the huddled masses, and the temple of the Spaniards. A sea of faces gathered outside, those like him, impure within the eyes of the Spanish and therefore barred from entering the Holy grounds on this day. But Surem didn't come to set foot upon the grounds of the Christ-Child. Instead he descended into the empty cellars below, to the foundations of the temple which lay beneath in total darkness. The chambers of the miniscule labyrinth were empty and Surem groped through the dense silence that contained the hushed memories of the old gods. Their sterile presence seemed to guide Surem along, retracing those steps he had already taken, a preordained trajectory, returning him to the small arch and the stone that lay at the center of the old temple. His calloused palms hovered over and then stroked the cold walls until his fingertips finally touched upon the stone arch. His hands ascended to the top, to the apex where the triangular center-stone lay, the peak of the arch, and the granite felt tiny and fragile against Surem's palms. He sensed something after a few moments within the stifling black, a steady thrum and vibration emanating from the three points of the stone, like the hushed breaths that must precede life. Here were those memories, the forgotten records of the past, a transcription of everything that had been lost to the amnesiac hands of time, a promised renewal, salvation, his grandmother's salvation. It had only been three days yet he longed to see her again, to swim in the vision of her blue eyes. That's all he could remember of her with any intensity, blue eyes, calm, cool, the opposite of this boiling earth.

He dug his fingers into the cracks of the arch and clawed, pulling with his remaining strength. The stone remained placid, unaffected by the calloused hands around it. Surem kept pulling with taut shoulders and forearms, muscles which were accustomed to toiling in the ancient gravel, now yanking at this stone, wrenching the past from its subterranean roots, bringing it to light once again. And then it moved, in increments smaller than the invisible steps of the moon across the sky, and he could feel the stone almost loosen, and through the blind darkness he heard an inhuman echo growing, as though a deep chasm was opening and the dead gods were yawning at the bottom.

The stone finally broke free, yet after a few moments it did nothing, only a dead weight in Surem's hands. But the space it had come from, the apex and center of the arc, slowly became illuminated by something more pure than light. He peered into the empty, negative space and his pupils were bombarded with an onslaught of phantoms, apparitions, images. They appeared unsuccessive, simultaneously, in a single instant, but an instant that covered the solemn abyss across infinity, like a shattered crystal dragged through every point in time, then reassembled into a new prism with the images reflected through each fragmented piece, and he saw it all with an unwavering gaze: the roots of a cacti, a naked child paddling in the ocean, the stroke of a bird's wings, clouds, rains, a land of ever-changing dunes, boats filled with people darker than shadows, eyes staring through a slit in purple cloth, temples hidden beneath a sea of green vines, a bleeding coyote, hands inscribing a foreign yet beautiful language, flooded roads, dry voices, boulders tumbling into water, water droplets falling from frozen leaves, insects flying, insects crawling through the skeletal frame of a dead bird, men clashing, wood and metal and stone piercing flesh, the silent atrocity of a child frozen in ice with its eyes still wide-open, the breadth of a starving hunter, arrows that miss their mark, cities of pure light, fire, smoke, burnt flesh, lesions of the skin, a mother's hands, women with painted faces, oceanic waves, a tapestry of setting suns, the first light to pierce through the creosote branches, the vacant spaces between the sands of the desert…

Amidst all he saw, all those pristine images, he noticed a solitary figure pulling a child from a massive pile of rubble. The lonesome figure had eyes reminiscent of a cold, leafless winter. The figure's long jawline and overbearing brows were familiar to Surem, a face he had only glimpsed in the pale reflection of clear waters, a face he knew, a face he recognized as his own. The other eyes, the child's, were those of his grandmother's, he knew instantly. A bleeding scar was freshly carved into the child's cheek. Surem watched the figure—himself—take the child's hand and they left the rubble and continued past a mass of injured people in a dusty village, voyaging into the open expanse.

The two—Surem's reflection and the child—crossed through the desert sands with thirsty mountains looming in an unreachable horizon. During the cold and indifferent nights the two huddled close together, their bodies kept warm by one another and nothing else. They finally made it out of the desert after many days, their path leading them to another tribe, people of the endless sands, like themselves, others who knew the hardships of a ceaseless sun. The two wanderers were welcomed into the village and the child grew older between dried-mud walls. And Surem saw the figure's face—his own, a phantom of himself—keep a steady gaze upon the blue-eyed child, caring for her, teaching her a new language, urging her to forget her slithering Castilian. As the child matured her skin darkened to the landscape, but her eyes always remained like droplets of the sky. She learned to heal, to make medicines, to mix remedies perfectly, to amplify the healing nectars found across the land. The solitary figure—his pale reflection, his ghost, his echo—loved the child. Even when the child grew sick, a small cough, a fever, and the child survived the sickness, but the illness took others, ravishing the village, a cough, a lesion of skin at first, a disease which crept steadily through the town, lurching, always hungry for more. The plague had arrived and death left nothing untouched with her spectral fingers which slid down throats and gradually choked the life from all those infected. The child had brought the sickness to the people, she was the harbinger of the plague, her sins lay within her foreign blood, blood that boiled across the sun-soaked lands, blood that made her the mother of the plague.

Years later, during one fragile night, the reflected figure—Surem's own—abandoned the child and followed the light of the moon to live a solitary existence on the outskirts, across the borderlands. Alone, the figure grew tall, his voice deepened. He learned to only trust the call of the coyotes, the scents they picked up, their primal instincts that remained intimately attuned with the desert. His eyes absorbed every passing frigid winter and his ears were haunted by the chorus stuck in the wind, the voices which sang to him of reminisces and remembrances, of memories and sins that could never settle into the desert sands.

Then the instant of kaleidoscopic images ceased and Surem returned fully to the darkness of the subterranean chamber. He knew what he had seen, the memories that hadn't solidified into the past, memories that were yet to unfold. He inhaled the sublime horror of knowledge, of a certainty that contained every possibility and excluded nothing, the preordained and reoccurring finality that perpetuated itself through him. It was a glimpse of his origin, the architecture that condemned him from its inception, a prison of reoccurring time.

A guttural roar issued forth form the blackness, the earth shook as though it had been cleaved open to its very core, to the center where the void lay within everything. His mind stumbled over itself and wondered if this was the cry of the old gods, of those buried and forgotten, the roar of those who found a bit of life for a moment and were now dying a second death. Warm breaths of a monolithic, unseen specter descended upon his skin, chasing him as he ran from the labyrinth, his body slamming into hardened walls, scrambling, until he finally caught sight of light, ascending, up towards the sunlight, finally reaching the open air and loose gravel ground.

The roar and visceral tremors continued amongst masses of bodies trying to escape disintegrating walls. The foundations had collapsed and now the Spanish temple imploded upon itself. The two-crossed lines atop the Spanish *iglesia* fell and finally rested upon the barren earth alongside the rest of the collapsed structure. The tremors slowly throbbed and disintegrated into the silent horizon, and all that remained was a pile of rubble, fragments, debris which Surem recognized, ruins he had already seen, a wreckage which he witnessed once again, a catastrophe he had remembered from a time before.

Strong and calloused hands pull you into the full glare of the sun. Your light-blue eyes shutter in pain, but you are free, your frail body is no longer trapped within the consuming black. You focus on the man holding you and you notice a sincerity in his brown eyes, but they also seem cold, as though they were made in the purest of winters. Your slender fingers move towards the pain upon your face and for the first time you feel the bleeding gash upon your head. You begin to cry but the man holding you in his powerful forearms hushes you in a language you cannot comprehend, words that mean everything and nothing in equal measure. His voice is a voice you might have heard once before, but you are not sure because you cannot remember anything, only the blind, roaring tremors that held you, incubated you, then birthed you to the world. The man takes you away from the rubble which you recognize, if only vaguely. You struggle to pull from the negative spaces of your mental landscape—are you reborn, or is it that you've died again and this is yet another life, a different one, one with another name, another voice—and then you hear it, yes, something is there, you hear it within the crevices of your soul, the faint echo of voices that you might have dreamt once before in another life.

THE RIBBONS

by Ferguson Williams

Poppa overheard Paul-Ann from his position on the porch. "Shhh… D'yall hear that?" she said. And for a moment they all looked up from the fields, Mama and Jillian and Emma, expecting to see coming up the road the band of tired motley n****** who'd run off days before. He raised the rifle just in case someone was coming but only the wind approached, blowing across the women on their hands and knees as they picked the last of the turnips to cook for supper. That was all there would be tonight. Nothing in the earth seemed to last. "I hear Pammy sangin'. It's Pammy comin' home."

So they all tried to hear what the youngster heard but they couldn't. He knew Mama didn't have the heart to tell Paul-Ann about the escaped slaves going wild, killing white people over in Ogdenville, raping Christian women and destroying everything in their path like locusts. Instead she told the child the slaves would return. They'd see that there was nothing for coloreds out there. The world was a harsh and scary place and they'd had a good life living on the manor. The slaves owed them thanks for that. Besides Pammy would be so lonesome she'd come running back.

For the life of them, he and Mama and Jillian and Emma couldn't hear a thing. The fact that Paul-Ann could and seemed so delighted in the return of her precious Pammy scared Mama so bad that Mama made them abandon the few turnips they hadn't picked and head inside immediately.

He was still standing guard as the women made their way back to the house. Their pace was steady, almost graceful, but as they ventured closer he saw no grace only truth. Jillian and Emma were barely of courting age yet their rosy skin and flaxen hair once envied were gone. Circumstance seemed to have aged them overnight; their features hardened by uncertainty. Frocks that once clung to every curve tempting every suitor now looked like cast offs on an old scarecrow.

Young Paul-Ann trailed behind her sisters, wandering in and out of line, apparently oblivious to the current state of affairs. A bout of malaria years

ago had slowed her mentally, allowing her now to detach and reattach to reality whenever she wanted. He often pitied her being so beautiful and yet so simple minded, 'special' Mama called her, but right now he almost wished he could trade places with his daughter. To escape from the grayness of this situation, this life, this misery even for a moment would be...

In the rear of the group marched his wife, his dear sweet wife who faked a placid smile in his direction. Yet the fear in her eyes betrayed her, offering him a glance that made him feel obtuse.

They should have left when the others did.

"Slim pickin's, eh?" It was all he could think to say as his family brushed past with their tattered dresses and disheveled hair. No one answered as they went inside.

Paul-Ann lingered though, looked over her shoulder back towards the fields and said, "Pammy be here soon, Poppa. She comin' to make thangs right and she will too, uh huh. Jus' you wait and see." He ushered the girl inside nervously, latching the door behind him. With the Winchester cradled in his arms like a baby, he began repositioning the cupboard to block the entrance.

It wasn't until dusk that they all heard it too, a sound so faint and low at first that it seemed to travel on the wind. It tumbled over the pond and the sycamore trees that lined its edges. It swept across the lawn of their modest plantation and crashed at the foot of the porch steps. It journeyed slowly up the wooden planks, rocked his old rocking chair, and scratched at the front door like an old tom cat looking to come inside. Then there was darkness. A purplish black haze enveloped the house so fast that the birds, huddled in the trees, went squawking towards the heavens.

He looked back at Mama for confirmation that she heard the noise as well. He motioned to her to extinguish the fire, but Mama seemed too frightened to look in his direction, let alone do anything. He whispered her name.

The older girls seated in front of the roaring flames murmured, "Mama," but she still didn't respond.

Paul-Ann laughed and clapped her hands. He gazed at her, his face rigid. "Hush." He parted the curtains with the barrel of his weapon. There was nothing out there even though he could clearly hear singing. He knew it wasn't Pammy, for Pammy had hung weeks ago from a tree down by the creek. But it was someone, a group of someones, singing a song he'd often heard the niggers sing in the fields.

"Red, red ribbon, it gon' be alright.
Red, red ribbon, jus' stay in the light.
Red, red ribbon be on everythin',
For the blood of Jesus Christ gon' wash away all sin."

Paul-Ann began shouting, "I tol' y'all Pammy was comin'. She here, she here. Come on in, Pammy."

Mama, suddenly out of her trance, walked over and smacked the child right across the face. "Stop it now, Paul-Ann. Jus'... just stop it." Mama's voice was tense as she wrung her hands together over and over.

The young girl smirked in response to her mother's unusual ferocity and began singing, her voice somewhat off key and out of sync with those coming from outside. "Red, red ribbon be on everythin'."

Something heavy rolled across the porch, scaling the wooden laths like keys on a piano. Mama looked opaque, her teeth clinched. Paul-Ann clapped her hands and giggled like a babe. Jillian and Emma sat petrified. Only their eyes moved, darting from window to window following the singing. The noise settled in front of the door and the older girls began to whimper like puppies.

He moved, silencing his daughters' cries with a single finger held to his lips. He waved to get Mama's attention and, without a sound, commanded she get the Colt from the dining room table. She picked up the firearm like a live snake, as if it wiggled uncomfortably in her petit hands. He knew immediately that she would be useless.

The voices outside sang loud and strong.

"Get," he ordered. "Get on from here. Ya, ya not welcome and I, I don't want no trouble."

The song continued as if they didn't hear him.

"I been good to ya'll. I, I ain't never-"

The crooning sustained.

"Dammit, I will kill ya. Every one of ya. I

swear to God I will." There was no response to his calls, but someone touched the door knob, and startled, he fired towards the motion hitting the window. The glass and curtains exploded outward and in rushed the sound as if an entire church choir crossed into the parlor.

"Red, red ribbon-" The singing was clamorous. Jillian and Emma scrambled to their feet with hands capped over their ears and fled towards their mother.

Only darkness waited on the other side of the broken window. Not someone or a group of someones, just darkness. He looked dolefully back at Mama who tried to shield the older girls with her embrace. Mama was screaming something. The singing was just too loud and he couldn't hear but her face said it all. *John, do something before it's too late.*

A heavy breath parted his lips. He raised his gun and fired.

The Winchester bullet caught the crown of Mama's head. Clumps of hair and scalp burst back towards the wall. The girls screamed as their mother's body dropped to the floor like a discarded rag doll. He fired at Jillian and missed which gave the girl the opportunity to sprint to the staircase. Emma followed but her father's next shot caught her in the middle of her back, jerking her violently forward then crashing her head into the bottom step.

He eyed Paul-Ann dancing and singing by the table. She looked to be oblivious to the chaos, her mother and sister dead on the floor. With his sadness turning to anger, he cocked the rifle. Seeming to sense what was coming, the girl ran to the exposed opening and dove head first into the night, landing with a thud on the wooden porch.

"I tol' 'em you was comin', Pammy," she cooed as the sweet music swaddled her like an infant, blanketing her in darkness. And then she was gone.

"Red, red ribbon, it gon' be alright.
Red, red ribbon, jus' stay in the light.
Red, red ribbon be on everythin',
For the blood of Jesus Christ gon' wash
away all sin."

The requiem flooded the first floor like a mighty river. He moved with purpose: first to his wife's body to retrieve the Colt, then to the base of the stairs where Emma lay motionless. In time with the music, he leapt two and three steps at once until he reached the second floor. On instinct, he went to his wife's sitting room and there Jillian was, huddled next to Mama's old bureau.

Before he even raised the barrel of the gun she whined, "Poppa, please." He paused for a moment. Her eyes, her beautiful big brown eyes were those of her mother. Maybe there was a way. Maybe they could climb down the awning and... but then he heard them. The slight suction sound of their bare feet ascending the hardwood steps.

Something in his eyes must have told the girl there was no going back, that this was the end. She kicked at his legs in an attempt to keep him at bay. He was trying to save her from them. Why didn't she understand that? He placed the muzzle close to her chest as she lashed at him violently, screaming at the top of her lungs, "No, Poppa. No, Poppa."

He pulled the trigger.

"Puh... pa." Her mouth moved as if she were lost in thought, like she was singing a song she'd forgotten the words to. Tears cut tracks in the blood on her cheeks. Her head drooped to one side. Her chest moved once and a look of calm washed over her face. Her chest moved again and she was gone.

And he was alone with the someones whose footsteps were on the second floor. He could hear the creaking hinges of the bedroom doors down the hall as they opened one by one. With the rifle by his feet and the Colt to his temple, he mumbled a prayer then pulled the trigger.

Nothing. He pulled the trigger a second time. Still nothing.

He fell back into his wife's rocking chair and shook his head in disbelief. What she had told Paul-Ann was right after all. They had come back. They were singing low now, marching rhythmically down the hall, searching every room to find their master.

PERMUTATIONS

by Laura Cesarco Eglin

A sticker for another sticker became
a passion for a drawer for trash.
Recycling happens on the tip
of my fingers where I still feel
the fuzzy caterpillars, the glossy
fairies. My two hands
curl when in danger, guarding
my fingertips as much as inwards
is inside. I exercise them passing
those tips over surfaces to stream
cores like slicing melons and finding
fruit in your teeth. I force my fingers
over what's rough, let them bleed.
It only hurts if the red doesn't
stain. Blood for another day.

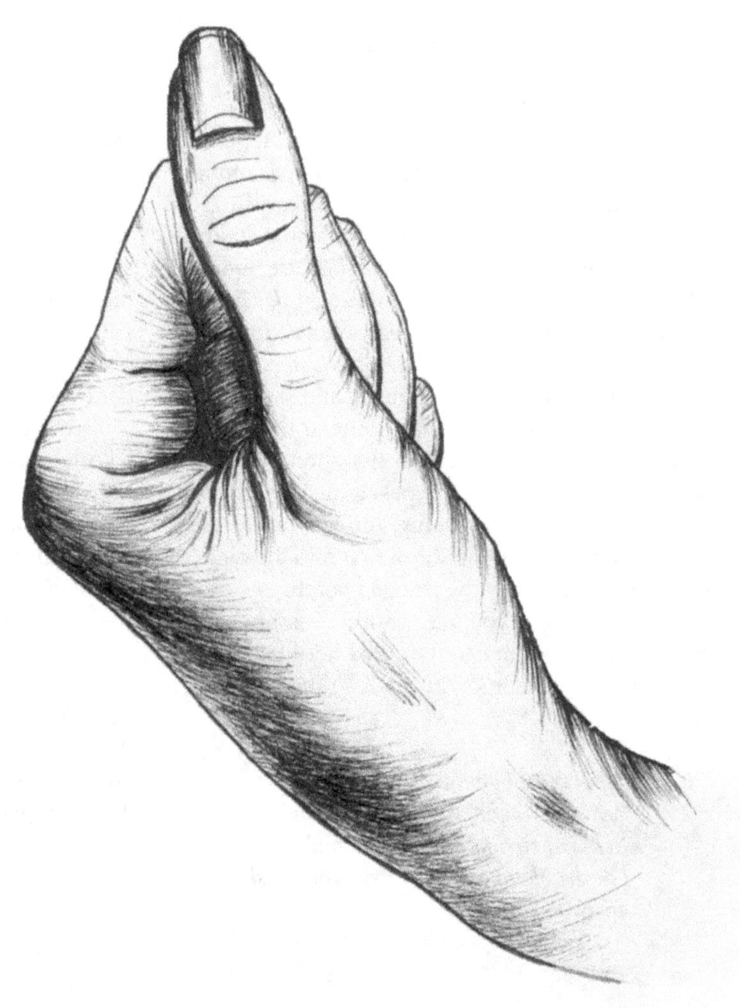

WITH THYME

by Laura Cesarco Eglin

I'm trying to catch what runs
as fast as the river. I wait.
Breath happens
regardless of what the mouth is
doing. To me
it runs until it changes direction
until it's time and time is all the time
intervening in the process of cooking
and compulsion. To have it be
inside. Returning to what
ran away what stopped
when I breathed.

LISTENING

by Laura Cesarco Eglin

I'm trying to hold my breath
one word at a time. Silence is
too subtle to let it speak all
at once is slower when it comes
to discerning what is not heard.
Quiet is in the tongue
that subsides to language.

WARDENCLIFF

by Barbara Daddino

A proposal:

Suppose, reader, on a cool summer day, you descended a long wooden stair that led through a bluff to a beach - call it Wardencliff - in search of, say a hag, who is rumored to live in a cave by the shore…

And I, a blind woman and a fool, but supposing myself to be said hag, heard your footfall on the pebbles as you stepped off the stair…

I would hide.

You, having seen, perhaps, a flash of white hair, a flap of black fabric might call out.

I listen as your unransomed calls fade, deliciously, in the sea.

Perhaps you persist. You might walk toward the boulder where I wait crouched, barely breathing, my cheek pressed to cold granite, mated to it. I listen as your step slows, as a stone you accidentally kick skitters over the sand and strikes the boulder behind which I hide.

Maybe you stop. You wait for a sound that would signal my presence.

And in this pause, this empty but electrified silence we have created between us, my heart quickens. Flattening my back, I rise along the boulder's wrack-damp wall. After some moments, your footstep resumes. As you draw near, the vein in my neck begins to throb like a lizard's. I wait until you *are* near, so near I can hear, not only your footfall, but the sound of your breath. And when I am sure that it is your breath, only then do I step from behind the rock.

The creature that has emerged before you, whether human or hag, is a grotesque. The hair, yellow-white, salted stiff like dried cod; the skin, windworn, deeply creviced. She - for you've determined this much - is bone-thin, and taller than you may have supposed. The clothing, the dark fabric you had seen, is not so much black, you discover, but colorless. A collection of loose, tattered fibers you cannot call *clothing*. It is simply a covering. But it is the eyes, yes, the eyes, I am sure of it, that stop you, for they have neither pupils nor irises. Plates simply, sandblasted clean. Blank corneas that gleam in the head, twin mirrors that reflect the sea and the fog.

Thus, I stand before you, nose keen, ear pitched, straining, for my part, to learn something of *you*: to catch your scent, to sense your body, to feel its heat, to know the amount of air you displace, trying by the tilt of my head to capture your startled expression in my mirror-eyes so that you may read it for yourself, and reading, become further alarmed. I am radar. I scan for fear.

On the other hand, you may determine that what stands before you is nothing more than a fool, and so you may turn, walk away, perhaps shaking your head...

Or would you take pity on me? You might begin, *Ma'am*…? [Ha! *Ma'am*. Rags, bones and the stench of urine - *Ma'am*! But then, ma'am, madam, my dear madman. Yes. I allow it. Stet.]

Ma'am, your hesitant probe might continue, *is anyone with you? Such a long way back. Do you need help with the stairs? I could give you my arm...*

[Here you are cloying, conflicted. You hope I refuse, but decency compels you to go on.]

The steps are awful, you say. *You take your life in your hands.*

[Guilt.]

Were you to go on this way, I would give you my back. And you, having been released from an unwanted obligation, would leave wondering, as you walk away, if you had indeed encountered the hag you had sought. Thus would we preclude anything that might have passed between us. Dissolution by mutual consent.

On the other hand, there is the possibility that we continue together. But for that to occur, we would need some new element to bind us, something of common interest. A house, say. Suppose there were a house on the bluff behind us. A bluff that is nearly eighty feet high. A tired Victorian: worn-white clapboard, sagging black roof. As you turn, it catches your eye. Can you see it there at the top of the bluff? Its turreted porch, its gabled roof? Not a large house, a cottage, really. Something that, were it smaller, might have been termed a *folly.* Maybe a blanket hangs drying over the rail or a tabby cat has jumped down from the porch swing. Perhaps a potted hydrangea stands tilted against a pile of loam. At the rim of the bluff, a low rainbow might float in the mist where a ticking sprinkler waters the lawn. All these things point to the fact that the house is inhabited, and yet, as with abandoned buildings, every window facing the Sound is covered over with two wide boards and a cross plank. It makes one wonder - that wonderful view, blocked. Why? The absurdity of it may even suggest a connection between me and the house.

Margaret's house, I answer before you ask. I hadn't meant to speak. The words leapt from my mouth of their own accord.

If I were to turn from you then, having realized that I spoke unprompted, idiotically... Or if you were to withdraw, as would be reasonable, as one would do, say, from a stray dog, hoping that it wouldn't follow... that would end it, this shared construct, this nascent story that is still teetering on the conditional. You would retreat to the safety of your own world and take with you an incident, a tiny mystery with which you would amuse your friends: *Do you know what I saw today at the beach? An old woman. A loon, really. Strange though, because...* Aah!

But what if you don't shrink from me? What if, instead, you reach, as one would reach, to turn the page of a book, and breaking with all decorum, you touch my hand? What would happen then?

As with light, I am at once flooded with the feel of you - the flesh, the bone, the warmth of your touch, the act of another intelligence upon me and I do not let go. No. I clamp my hand over your wrist, hold you by any means possible. I take on the guise of a helpless, hapless soul in order to draw you in. I pretend to be stranded (though this beach is a habitat so intimate, so much a part of me that should I be removed from it, it too, would disappear.) As you guide me (so you think) toward the beach stair, I explore the hand you have offered and feed on its warmth, while inside I am reeling with joy, reveling in the rainbow-colored dampness we share between the hollows of our palms. It has been years since I've felt the thrill of a human touch.

Picture us, can you, stumbling hand-in-hand over the rocks, through the sea mist and the gull cries, the rhythmic wash of water? And you, good soul, have no idea that what you hold onto, what you guide with your sweet and human hand is neither a fool, nor a hag, but a negative.

Perhaps at the foot of the bluff we pause to look up together at the boarded house. Through your grasp, I test the effect its blank gaze has upon you. I feel questions assembling and spreading like ink through your brain until you shake yourself free. Before we walk on, I glance at my cave, a cavity formed by a fortunate assemblage of fallen tree trunks and rocks that lies directly under the house, a shelter too unobtrusive for you to have seen.

At the beach stair you drop my hand. I listen. Perhaps there comes a clambering which I interpret as you climbing the steps. I assume you are going on without me. This, I think, is perhaps for the best, but then I am stunned by your hands gripping my wrists.

The bottommost step, you explain, is unsafe. You direct me to raise my foot high, to place it, not on the first, loose step, but on the second. You hold onto me as I climb. A comfort, the return of your grip. A sweet and pure comfort.

And if you hadn't reached down to me, if you hadn't taken me by my wrists as you did, drawing me to you, pulling me to you; if together we hadn't climbed the long wooden stair that leads up through the bluff, our footsteps echoing our ascent on the boardwalk there; if we hadn't followed the thin sound of a cricket's chirp, then another and another until the chirps interwove in a network of song; and then continued, hand in hand, deeper and higher to where the boardwalk ends and a path of bare sand begins, a path that felt increasingly cooler and damper under our feet as it changed from sand to dark, loamy soil; and leaving behind the tall grasses and the beach plum, if we hadn't entered woods of locust and oak where thick vines of briar choked off the sea noise and the draped air grew hushed; if we hadn't climbed up still further winding our way through sun-shafts and birdsong until we came to that final steep flight of steps and having climbed them, walked across a car park and out through a gate onto a road, in order to stand, at last, in front of *her* house, I could have told you nothing about the house, about Margaret or myself.

Nor would you have found out. Suppose you had never come to the beach, never encountered me nor laid eyes on the boarded windows. Suppose, instead, you had come upon the cottage, just as we have now, by the road. Your eye might have been caught by a flutter of tulle through an upstairs window. Maybe you stopped to admire the clematis-cloaked mailbox, the rose-covered arch. You might even have smiled at the arched wooden door, at how the little house stands so earnestly among the oaks and the cedars believing itself to be a cottage. Gazing upon it, you would come to believe too. Standing here under sheltering trees, it is easy to believe in cottages. But the place is a counterfeit. The cottage, spellbound. And you would have been deceived by the rustle of leaves and honeysuckle air.

Eventually, you would walk on, but the cottage would haunt you, for it is an illusion you want to believe in. And the image would attach itself to you and lay embedded in your mind - as you converse over dinner, as the telephone rings, as you run a shower - returning full-force as you drop off to sleep. And all the time you would not suspect that what you had perceived as a haven stands at the edge of a crumbling bluff, exposed to cruel winds and a capricious sky.

Now as we stand here together in front of the house, look close. Lean on my memory while I, who am blind, sharpen your sight. There was once a wire fence - it is still there, isn't it? I'm sure it is. That element will not have changed. On the other side is a wooded lot. Do you see how new shoots of briar strain through the fence, towards air, towards light. Nearby, no doubt, a wild grapevine tightens around a sapling like a cord about a lover's neck. Wild raspberry bushes, stalky, unpruned, bend under the weight of fruit, and gaudy black pods of Solomon's Seal nod above sweet-smelling loam.

Now look toward the cottage. What in its yard is random, whorish, freely given? Margaret has hacked out the briar, rooted out weeds. The raspberries, if there are any left, have been clipped to a hedge. Those secretive blossoms, jack-in-the-pulpits and wild violets, are laid bare in massed plantings. In this contrived space even the birds are given houses; even the lilies reek of her hands.

I can tell you things. I've lived here a long time - as long as Margaret. That *is* the owner's name. Had I mentioned that? Forgive me, I've forgotten. She lives alone, as do I. But neither of us is really alone. Years ago when I was sighted I would watch her go to the stores and back, to the library and back, to the galleries and back - always returning with packages, always collecting. Things. Incessant. Still does. If anything, it's gotten worse. My eyes are useless now, but I can still listen. From my cave below I hear her going around in her garden planting this *indigenous* shrub, that new *woodland* plant. Day after day, her spade scrapes the soil. She plants grasses, sets trees, tunnels in. In her head, she has created a refuge, but for all of her efforts, her land still falls away.

I'm tired. I want to quit this place and slip back into my cave. I want to be rid of her, and rid of you, for that matter - you with your questions about those windows. However you did take my hand. You tagged the witch. I therefore I must pay a price. So before we part, I will pay my debt and tell you the reason Margaret has boarded her windows.

Running alongside the fence is a path. We will take it out to the crest of the bluff. Once there, I will tell you what you want to know. But I warn you, the path we will follow is steep and deceptive. Use balance, not eyes, for the incline will tempt you to lean. And if you do, you will lean out too far, sway, perhaps tumble... Ah well, come along. You'll discover that the air lightens as the path opens out to the sea.

We have emerged onto a shelf of bayberry and grass that extends like a crooked finger across the face of the bluff. Beneath our feet, ravines of running sand, bushes and trees set adrift on islands of soil broken off from above. About our ears, wind. Before us, sky. On the face of the bluff a few tufts of grass, poison ivy and grapevine survive. At the base, perhaps goldenrod, switch grass and spurge - no more than a season's growth. These bluffs bear the brunt of the north wind, suffer the hunger of the tide which, each winter, rises to gnaw at their base. Tiers of sand from above collapse to replace what had been drawn off below. In consequence, Margaret's garden dwindles by a foot each year. and her trees become undermined. They drop one by one from the cliff, and their cracked trunks are driven like pitchforks into the beach.

Erosion is the central fact around which our lives revolve. It makes sisters of us, and that is what terrifies her. It is not against erosion per se, but against our bond that she boards her windows.

Sometimes, late at night, when the wash of the tide licks at my ear, I turn in my cave, put my cheek to its cool, soft wall and listen to the stirrings of the earth. From all over the face of the bluff I can hear the sand loosening under a rock, trickling from a stump. For hours I listen to the rasping. Then comes the slide. Each fall is like a birth. And it's all so steady: the trickle, the slide, the wash of the sea. She has sealed herself off from the sounds of erosion, but they are the sounds I sleep by.

We have arrived at a new phase, reader. Do you feel it? A turn of the cog? A fitting into the slot? Or is it, rather, a modulation of sorts? But what can be left between us? I have answered your question about the boarded windows, and you have returned me to my bluff. Now that pledges have been kept, duties fulfilled what more can be left between us? Yet there *is* something - on your part, you may feel my story insufficient; as for me, I sense an impending intimacy, one for which I am unsuited, or at least, unprepared.

Listen. The sea-surge has quieted. There is only a weak, rhythmic collapse at the shore, and fog creeps like ghost-breath about us. On a day such as this, Margaret will surely come. She will come in her little boat. She will come rowing along the shore. She will set anchor before us, in line with the house. In line with my cave below it. A tarp will be hooding her head. Her face, pinched and white and haunted by dread. She will raise a small, brass telescope to her eye in order to check on the state of the bluff. What she will find in her lens is my image.

Will you wait for her then? We can sit here together on this shelf of bayberry. Let your feet dangle. Abandon your eyes. Let blind balance inform you. Meet her with me. Will you? Will you?

You are wearing binoculars. I heard them thump against your chest when we were walking, felt the heat of the lenses, sensed the strap chafing your neck. There was a time when I, too, wore them. When my eyes worked. Loved the weight of them, the response of the lens to my fingers, the ridges of the dial, the precision...

Do you see that tilting cedar - just to our left? Any day it will topple. Only a few roots still anchor it to the ground. The rest of the roots have lost their soil and hang mid-air. This is the province of gulls. They are always out there, gliding, diving. Far away one is shrieking. The response breaks over our heads. A sudden fluttering all about us, noise and movement gathering in the west. There must be by now a grainy form on the water, making its way through the fog. Has it materialized yet? Can you see it coming in our direction? Be my eyes and watch as the image takes shape, until you can see that it is, yes, a person in a rowboat, that it is she, that it is Margaret! Take up your binoculars. Train them on her. Tell me, does she appear to be struggling? Are the oars too long for her to handle? Is the water too heavy? Has mist matted her hair? Does water drip into her eyes? Or does she indeed wear a tarp? Is her bearing as miserable as I know it must be? Describe her to me, reader. Tell me. Tell me!

Gulls dip and scream around her like harpies. Their cries mark her progress for us. Listen, now, for the wash of the oars, the change of stroke, the pivot and backwash that stops the boat, and there - the hollow sound of oars drawn through oarlocks like dead limbs. The harrying gulls disband. Fog closes over their calls as the sky presses like a lover onto the sea. We, too, are sealed in that liquid breath, in vapors and swells. We are alike finally, you and I, the two of us fog-bound and blind.

Margaret must be raising her telescope and scanning the bluff. What is the state of her garden she wonders? How badly has that thin spit of soil been undermined? Has the cedar yet toppled? Has some branch or boulder [*Oh! please God*] stemmed for a while the streaming sand? I feel the sweep of her lens across my own mirror-eyes. The air is filled with her. She shudders and the air trembles. What sight has shaken her - the cedar that is about to topple, or my eyes?

Now is the time, reader, before she puts down her spyglass. Train your binoculars on her. Keep her pinned, your lens to hers. Hold her down while I drink her in. Let me swallow her. Yes, yes!

We three are braced. Bound by lenses and mirrors, and spinning together like elements stirred in a liquid suspension. Faster, still faster, until we reach such a speed that we rip through the fog. It splits like tissue and drifts away. Look, the sky is clear! So clear, even I can see, reader! And the Sound is a sharp and glittering blue. There are boats on the water - I see as a child might see them - rowboats and motorboats, clammers, and sailboats, their bright hulls and braided wakes and pennants fluttering against the blue.

This is the harbor of Gull Haven. I remember it just this way: the Victorian houses, their white porches and gables peeking through trees that line the shore; the rising hill that forms Main Street; the barber shop, the gift shop, the fish market huddled artlessly at its base. Across the street is the harbor itself opening to the Sound where the ungainly ferry is just now pulling in toward the shore. Next to the ferry dock is the town park with its huge oaks and gravel paths. The park benches with quilled iron sides line a section of shore.

The village continues to form in fogs the widening gash, a bright tableau floating between the waves and the sky. We see it all happening before our eyes. Margaret, in her boat, sees it too. She thinks she is watching a memory - but that is not so, not entirely. In the vision a young woman has just left the antiques shop on the corner. She crosses the street, a miniature shopping bag in hand. Pretty girl. Long chestnut hair. She looks to be eighteen or nineteen. Actually, she is twenty-four. Still young. Such a lively walk. Long stride, confident - or over-confident, would you say? One might imagine that she is consciously trying to make an impression - upon whom? An unseen admirer, or upon the world at large? She is not beautiful, but possessed of a tenuous grace, like the grace of an Afghan hound or a unicorn. The same incongruities. Our subject, of course, is Margaret at an earlier time in her life. A carefree disposition - wouldn't you say? The white paper bag swings from the girl's hand as she walks. Precious pink curling ribbons, moss green tissue paper. A gust of wind off the harbor blows back her rich chestnut hair. Sunlight slides along its strands.

- I was wearing pearl earrings.

Ah, a voice from the rowboat! The elder Margaret speaks.

- Always pearl earrings. Mikimoto, pink-tinged. A wonderful luster. I wore them every day.

She is indeed with us then - the Margaret-in-the-boat. As I have said, she regards this scene that has bloomed before us as memory. And, to an extent, that is true. But its immediacy arises from a penetration only my eyes can accomplish - the mirror flash that has parted the veil of time to admit, not only past events, but also possibility, for what my eyes have exposed is life in the process of happening. Though she doesn't realize it, I present Margaret-in-the-boat a terrible task: not only to watch with her current and life-scarred eyes how she denied the promise life had once offered, but to offer her that choice all over again. Poor dear.

So it is a contest, you see, between me and Margaret, a struggle neither of us is ever free of. To give you a sense of it, let me point out the young woman's earrings. Margaret-in-the-boat has it that the girl in our tableau, is wearing pearl earrings. Margaret's fabrication entirely. She has adorned the young woman with a symbol of supreme propriety. She has chosen white pearls, pasted them on those young earlobes as if with a glue-gun. Look back again at the younger Margaret who walks toward the park. She is alive, feeling at this very moment the brilliant sun upon her shoulders, upon her bare and slender arms, the sun that we three, as mere observers, cannot feel. Now, while the shore breeze ruffles the young woman's hair, and those long gleaming strands flicker across her ears, see for yourself what earring is there: a silver star. A simple five-pointed star. A cheerful and guileless star, the kind that is found on the flag, a piece of the Fourth of July glinting there on her right lobe. As she stops and bends down to admire a sidewalk planting of cosmos and cleome, she turns so that we see her full-face, the breeze rises and the other lobe appears. This one tenderly dented by a silver crescent moon. Not pearl earrings at all, but a star and a moon.

An affectation? In our eyes, surely. But let us be generous. She is young and can't yet tell the difference between the genuine and the disingenuous even in herself. She has had intimations that she is an artist - or that she has an artistic bent at the very least. So as she dresses for a day to be spent at seaside shops and art galleries, she spontaneously adds these earrings, a costume to reinforce her imaginative leanings. Shall we deem the mismatched earrings then a symptom of an unformed personality?

And so from this squabble between the elder Margaret and myself about which earrings our subject is to wear, a more fundamental issue arises: Who owns the story? Which set of earrings will stand? Who is to have the final say - Margaret-in-the-boat, or me? Each of us, after all, has a purpose. Margaret wants to confirm the correctness of her life's path. I want to torment her with all that her choice has denied.

Then too, it is possible something unexpected will occur... If the young Margaret, for instance, should intervene. If she were to take her fate in her hands. Characters may, in fact, become autonomous... But then even I sometimes hope against hope.

To move on - the miniature shopping bag Margaret carries. What is inside it? As yet, it is a mystery, but to the young Margaret who has chosen the contents, its appeal is so strong that she feels she has to see it again only minutes after purchasing it. Just now, she has entered the park and is seated on one of the benches along the harbor bank, undoing the curly ribbons of the bag, ripping them finally since they won't untie, and pulling out the moss green tissue paper, which she, despite her haste, takes the time to fold and to slide back down into the bag. She lifts out the trifle she has just bought. At first glance, it looks like an old print. It is, in reality, a framed playing card, a joker from a deck billed as "Depression Era." An odd illustration, one that has made a lasting impression upon her - a fool dressed in motley. He is sitting inside a soap bubble with his feet kicked up along the bubble wall. His body is posed sideways, but his head is twisted full-face to the viewer. His hair sticks out in wild red tufts from his belled cap. His grin is wide and cynical. One hand rests on a bent knee; the other holds a long, thin clay pipe. The bubbles he has blown, large ones and small, surround him, and he sits amid them in a bubble of his own, rising. Grinning and rising.

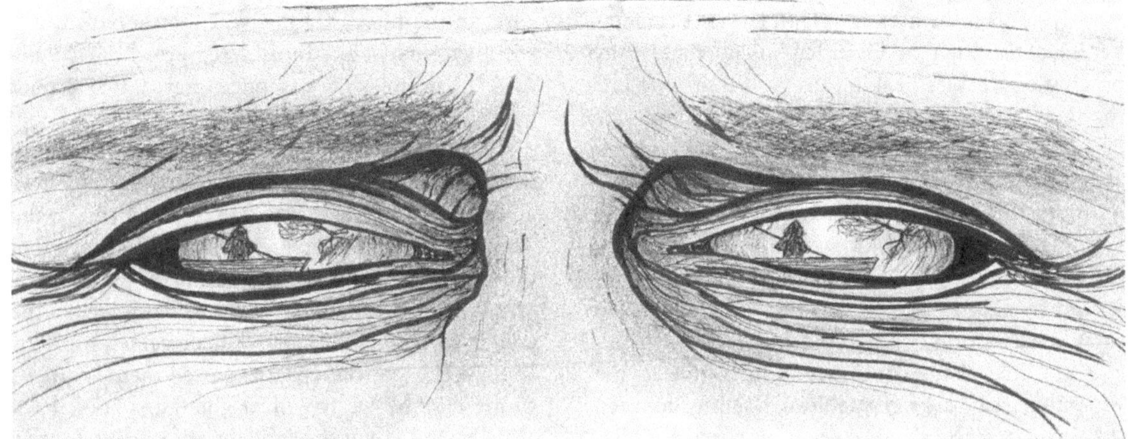

Who has put the card in the bag? Since it was purchased out of our sight and before our arrival, it must be something that appealed to the young Margaret, but what possible appeal could it have had, this jaded image, to one who is new to the world, who takes everything at face value, who is interested only in the flowers and geegaws of the little town? Might we have been deceived? Might it not be a sleight-of-hand of Margaret-in-the-boat... she who once felt the very same sun, breathed the same sweet air but who looks back upon the scene from the chill and the drear of where she now sits? Might she not have switched the article that the young Margaret actually purchased (scented candles or potpourri, perhaps) with this playing-card? Then again, what of me? I who have conjured the two Margarets in the first place? It is I who have been your principal guide. I depicted for you the house with boarded windows, lead you to this place on the bluff, burned with my blazing eyes this hole through the fog. Am I not the most likely candidate to have chosen the card? Neither shall I neglect you, reader, who are the occasion for the story. It was you who came to Wardencliff to seek me out. You, too, have brought your lens, and you shall play your hand in this odd contrivance we call a *tale.*

Forgive my digressions. It is time to move on. The time of seduction has passed. There has been a union of minds. The curtain has parted. Now a gestation, a percolation, if you will, like our fool's bubbles, rising, filling pages with image and incident. Or if you'd rather, think of it as frog spawn.

So. Let us assemble our imaginings and match wits. As to the rules of engagement, we will let Margaret-in-the-boat lead with her account. I will guide you through by adding my comments to her story. She is watching the tableau before us carefully, shifting her body to find the best angle. There, see the sunlight filtering through trees? It is Margaret who is pouring this honeyed light unto the scene to accompany her younger incarnation along the park's path. There now, as the girl makes her way, the one in the boat narrates - as if she were watching a home movie:

Yes, I remember the graveled path, the shaded lane that meanders towards the center of the park. Halfway through was a gazebo. I used to imagine the music of oom-pah bands, but I don't know if they ever really played there. The twin lines of oaks, the rustling canopy, the dancing light... They were so beautiful, those tall, full trees...

[Let her run on for a while with this saccharine narrative. Let her smear her descriptions over the scene like marmalade.]

...those full trees that had grown for generations unimpeded and beloved. On the lawn that day a teen-ager was playing Frisbee with his dog. Three little girls sat cross-legged eating ice-cream cones, giggling as I walked by. They looked up at me adoringly, the way little girls do at older girls.

[...says the wet mouse riding the swells. Her honied light illuminates for us what she would like us to think is the unimpeachable past. The boy and his dog, the two little girls, tongues curling about the dripping cones - halcyon images that we watch in silence from our perch.]

From out of nowhere, a drop of water splashed on my hand. Raindrops spattered suddenly on the leaves above me, one on my arm, more at my feet. It was a sun shower!

[The Mouse has begun to diverge. She is changing the story. There was no shower that day. So it begins. I'll play along. Let's see. What details might I add? Clammers that pause mid-stroke. Yes, that's good. See them appear before us, their forearms crossed over their long-poled rakes. They look up appraising the clouds and wonder...]

The little girls squealed and ran for cover. The boy wiped the wet Frisbee on his jeans and threw it again onto the sparkling grass, and the dog, pink-tongued and clownish, chased it down. Everything was wet. There was no point in staying, so I decided to leave...

[So this is what she's up to. She wants to make a quick exit, but I'll not let her run out on this - I'll intervene.]

It is only a passing cloud, young Margaret. Wait it out. Here's a bench.

Well, yes, there was a bench...

It is sheltered. Dry. [No excuse, now, Mouse, for your younger self to leave.]

...but the bench was taken.

There's room on it, child, for at least two.

The man sitting on it was a townie. Worker's clothes. Flannel shirt...

In the summer, Mouse? A tee-shirt, is more apt, don't you think?

Or if not flannel, linty, then. Untrimmed hair at the nape of his neck. Unsavory.

Still, you cannot deny that the young Margaret feels an attraction. Don't you remember, Mouse, how the hairs on your flesh rose?

Thinking back on it, he must have been young and attractive, but at the time he seemed an older man.

Eight years apart, would you say? Look at his hands, Margaret.

Vaguely threatening. He was holding a small block of wood and a knife.

His critical eye examines the wood. Closely. A bird over a worm.

He was turning the wood round and round in his hands, studying it. There was something about him. He was thin. Probably poor. Still, I would have to admit to a certain dignity in his hands, his long fingers and the grace...

Schooled fingers and interesting. Sit, sweet Margaret, and watch for a while. It's still raining, and this bench is sheltered. Something he does with the knife excites you. Sit, sit, for the whittling movements stir you in such a way - in the same way, Margaret, that I stir you, I who have always been with you, intimate as the blade of a knife.

Although his gaze was fixed on the wood, I felt uneasy. I felt he was watching me indirectly. I was uncomfortable and I might have left then... should have left.

What do you fear, Margaret? The knife? Then let your sister-hag take over the story a while... The rain stops. Sun is playing on his shoulders.

Yes, something warm about him and comfortable, the dappled sun on the fabric of his shirt. Maybe...

A twist of his wrist, now, as the blade cuts a slit in the wood and sunlight slides through the pinions of a bird's wing.

Maybe it was my shadow that made him look up. He did look up ...

He smiles at you, Margaret.

At this point, I might retreat from the tale as well as not, reader, for the young Margaret and the whittler have safely met. The Mouse-in-the-boat is quite capable of continuing the story on her own. She could, no doubt, recount quite accurately the twelve days they spent together. She might recall for you the time and place of their meetings, the weather, the words they spoke, the clothing they wore - all the commonplace particulars of the matter. What would be the point? What follows the whittler's smile is the simple progression of events that often occur when two people, young, unattached, are attracted to one another. They fall in love. Or think they do. They find themselves involved in a benign and uncomplicated affair - sweet sop. The stuff with which Margaret nourishes herself. He will go on about his *art,* he will mouth philosophies; she will use words like *brilliant, genius* perhaps. They will swear that they are closer than flesh. Who can say? Sex? Certainly. There will be the thumb across the lip, the tongue on the clitoris, the rubbings and chafings, the nip on the foreskin. Ah, me. The pet names, the nipple coaxings, the slick sheen smeared on unlikely places along with thin streams of sand and seaweed weavings and seashell decoration. The trading of scent. All of this is of no real importance. I will leave these details to the mouse. Yet I will tell you that what happens later is of real importance, for she will be led to a choice, and that choice is the reason I return again and again to the bluff, the reason I go through this exercise. For each time we recreate the story, she fails. And each time she fails, I drag her before these mirrors set in my head and I force to face what she's done. Call it a reckoning.

Look now as the tableau floats in the fog. See how the lovers play like children running and calling along the shore, this shore that is their constant meeting place, this Wardencliff above which we sit. They leap and trip over sand furrows, dance on beds of beach straw, sea wrack, shells and driftwood. And now, see where their shadows tilt intimately over a piece of translucent quartz. He holds it up to the light, forefinger and thumb bent around the stone. She puts her finger behind the rock and her finger is visible. A miracle - to see through stone. Their world is full of miracles. They eat wine berries, gaze out to sea. They decipher runes in the driftwood and laugh at the sandpipers' double-dutch at the shore.

What I give you of those first days they spend together are only fragmented images. I cannot recall each meeting individually nor can I recall certain details. I cannot, for example, remember the sound of his voice, that particular timber. Even his phrasing escapes me. How I once hung upon every word - for I was there with her. I lived within her. And she will not steal this joy from me - to savor life when we were vibrant and tender and whole. Though I am checked, now, and brittle, I will hang on. She will never be rid of me.

We rode bicycles along a private road, then onto a wooded path that led to the beach entrance.

The flash of sun on the bicycle spokes arcs and transforms time. You, Margaret, are entering that alternate realm visited only by lovers.

We hid the bikes behind briar. The lock on the beach gate was broken. Next to the gate was a sign, a long list of No's.

You and the whittler are trespassers here, children running hand in hand down the beach steps of Wardencliff.

We laughed at the ruler-makers. How they must have debated over the cause and prevention of litter, discussed bon-fires without permits, and dogs that might wander... Who, in their concerns, had forgotten the conchs and the sea wrack, the drift-wood and quartz, and the sun-tipped wings of the gulls.

At the bottom of the steps, the two of you pause to fill your greedy eyes with the ruffling blue sea, the pale, aching length of beach.

We spent some time skimming rocks on the water.

You wove seaweed through his hair.

He found a brownish-red rock, a paint pot he called it. He raised the sediment inside it with seawater, and with the ink he drew a line on my brow

Over the bridge of your nose

and another line on each cheek. Then I took the stone and traced

he colors your lips red and kisses them.

a long snaking line down his chest, below his navel, inside his thigh.

He takes your breasts in his hands, licks and kindles the nipples.

I thought we would make love then. Instead, he closed my eyes with his fingers.

The wind takes your hair.

He brushed the hair from my face,

And follows the curve of your neck,

his touch was too cool on my flesh...

"Come with me," he whispers.

... and his gaze slid past me.

The whittler leads Margaret eastward along the beach. The two stop directly under this spot where you, reader, and I are now perched. Look down. Do you see them emerging from the tableau? They are present at this very moment and real just below us. The whittler looks up in our direction. He does not see us, for we are in separate realms - but he points to the tree, the leaning cedar above us. Taking hold of her hand, he leads the young Margaret up the bluff guiding her, teaching her, despite her awkwardness and fear, to play with elevation and gradient, to tip and to lean, to love altitude and, turning back, to love the descent. They take long, bounding strides going downward, tilting backward from their knees, finding their center of balance, skidding on rivers of sand that rise and trail from their heels like moon-dust. Then they turn and climb up again. Breathless, they stop and rest on a shelf of sand just a few feet from where we now sit.

On that last day we sat high on the bluff watching the gulls skate across the sky.

Always and now: the gulls' cries, the shore wash, the reed rush...

We sat on the bluff for a long time wrapped in our own sea-washed silences.

...and all around, the knitting bayberry branches,

and wrapped, too, in each other's arms. At some point he locked my eyes with his.

He takes her wrists in his and leads her to stand.

and held me close. Then

With his touch, oh Margaret, which I can still feel...

he put his lips beside my ear

...this lizard heart warms, and my parched skin grows supple

his voice lured me into a vision,

as if I bask upon a sunlit leaf.

And he began, "There we will sit upon the rocks...

With those gentle words the young Margaret leans into the whittler's arms

"...A belt of straw and ivy buds

as his whisper enters and warms her like liquor.

"Come live with me and be my Love."

See how gently he slides off her shirt;

And it seemed to me as he spoke

his breath like a frond.

that I was both spirit and flesh,

Her long hair flutters and catches on the briar rose.

and as I clung to him I thought somehow...

Kneeling, he pushes the bayberry aside to make a space in the sand

...that I, too,

and eases her down.

might lead a life... that I might go with him...

The mingling scents of the sea and the roses and love.

After making love, they sit huddled together. He reaches over to her

He put a hand on my stomach,

and looks at her as one would read the pages of a book.

with the other, he lifted me by my forearm..

His seed stirring inside her....

We stood at the edge of the bluff; I was afraid of the crumbling crest, but he said, "Don't look down. Look ahead. Give yourself to the wind. Go where it takes you." I wanted to do it. I wanted to feel free and alive, but I laughed and kissed him instead. He looked down at his hands then and said, "It's the wind I carve, not the wing."

She rises to stand and the wind comes alive. His continuing voice washes over her like the tide carving a corridor to her deepest place, awakening the spirit that has lived there all along. His voice, along with the beach light, the wind, the sea - all of it whittling her, paring her; and all the time I am waiting within, coaxing her, singing, singing.

I saw above me the clouds rushing across the sky and below, their reflection scudding over the sea.

Her eye traces the line of a gulls' flight, a jet's trail, a deer's footprints in sand, a boat's wake - all the lines drawn by every order of things as if they are stating their mission - the streaks of carbon in granite, the beach grass rolling with the wind, the tide running along shore. Pattern after pattern opens to her, and it seems that each could be assigned a symbol, a punctuation mark or a musical notation - yes! And she can read chords and hear echoes and construct the earth's song and with it, finally, her own soul's song. This is the stream that runs through her, the life that stirs in her, the song I once sang to her. The song, reader, I offer her still.

Even now...

[Says the she still wearing the tarp.]

... I struggle with a desire to be something other... How can I explain it? That there is something else. Something I vaguely remember. It's like when a gull rises up from a boulder out in the Sound, tucks its feet into its chest, tents its wings and circles over the water - I long to go with it, I wish I could lift and lean on that wind and wheel over the the sea. I think for a moment I can grasp what the whittler meant.

And this is when I have reason to hope. See how below us Margaret stands in her boat. Bareheaded suddenly, she lifts her arms to the sky. Against her still-lovely neck, the sea's steady air. Her whole body feels it, and I continue to croon. My song entering, ripening, opening her like a husk. Meanwhile, the young Margaret watches the gulls. For the first time in her life, she is able to take on their glide and their power. She edges out to the rim of the cliff...

But then his meaning escapes me. Why was I standing so close to the edge? I might have been swept away.

A shudder like the wall of a bubble.

A gust of wind brought me to my senses. A gull hovered for a moment and hung so close I could have reached out and touched it. How clearly I saw the strain of its wingbeat. It's craning neck. Its feral gaze. In that flat eye I saw my own image reflected and trapped.

And so the trump card is played.

There is the hooked yellow beak that hangs over my boat. I think of him whose arms I once leaned into. I see again the ragged fingernail, the worn flannel shirt, the beads of sweat that formed on his lip. A artist's gaze, too, is indifferent and feral. I was not fooled by his scavenger eye. What had he offered really? And how much more had he meant to take?

See how the Mouse drops into her seat. The rowboat wobbles, and the younger Margaret looks down at her toes. With this single self-conscious act, a rock shifts, the rim she stands on begins to crumble.

He was a dreamer, a whittler, after all, and his arms no more a than a falling-away bluff... It was a madness. A madness.

As the slide quickens under her, she loses her balance. She does not take his hand that is outstretched to save her. Instead she reaches for a tree limb, which cracks. One of her legs slides down the bluff, but as she falls, she leans and tumbles onto our perch. From here, she manages to scramble back up and run, blind with fear away from the whittler, away from the bluff, to where her cottage now stands.

Even before the slide, I felt the quake of her fears, and I shuddered with dread. I knew I had lost, so I slipped away. A separate creature entirely, I watched her run off as the sand coursed around me. Then, from above, there came a terrible groaning of tree limbs. The tree she had grabbed for toppled over the bluff and I was trapped.

Sand sifted through the branches and briar that held me. It stopped up my ears and filled my eyes. I tried to blink it away, but it kept coming. Hour after hour of running sand. Sometimes a trickle, sometimes a downpour. I was pinned face up as my eyes were scoured, and in a kind of a trance, I gave myself to the rasping.

I was finally awakened... by quiet... by seawash. I remember the scent of crushed leaves, and the chill of night air. I managed somehow to get free and climb down to the beach. Caked with mud and blood, I lay down at the shore and let the tide wash over me. I emerged from the water as if I'd been hatched.

The fog has lifted, reader, and a pale sun has fallen upon us. It is a weak, uncommitted warmth, indifferent to my cold shoulders. It does, however, throw enough light for Margaret to see what she has come for - the undermined ledge, the cedar that will soon tumble. She is gratified, I think, more than fearful. When she gets home, she will do what she can - anchor the tree, put up a wattle embankment. She will take measures. But I welcome the trickling sand. My eyes are polished by it. See how brightly, how truly they shine! Look into them, reader. Examine carefully all that you see and tell me, who is the hag you seek?

Margaret has put down her lens and drawn up her oars. With the very first stroke, our story wrinkles and sinks in the raveling wake. You, too, will go now, and with your departure, I will fade into never-ness. But oh, reader! had I a knife and the skill of a whittler, I would carve a pipe out of driftwood, dip it into the sea, and fill the night sky with bubbles. In the largest of them I would rise... rise all the way up to her boarded windows where I would float and listen as each bubble pops.

The End

MIRAGE, OKLAHOMA

by Mark P. Lawley

---

1. A day in Lawton-Fort Sill

By dawnlight, the town is a fever dream of highway mirages, clapboard houses, and dusty streets full of strays. Traffic moves at the pace of daydreams along grid roads, going from neighborhoods laid out like barracks to perfectly rectangular plazas. The military personnel make the town possible, and they have been stationed here and not elsewhere for reasons obscure. Lawton: the violent incarnation of a college town, where honor hangs so heavy in the air that a wrong look can lead to a family feud, that honking your horn in traffic is challenging a man to a duel.

By high noon, the mirages unleash water into every rise and fall of the streets; they shimmer like jet engine exhaust out on the bare red fields, and we drive in the 100-degree illusions. G.I.'s and marines spend their paychecks in restaurants, massage parlors, strip clubs, strip malls, and Walmart. The civilians of Lawton work at these places or fulfill a serviceman's needs in some indirect way, at some satellite of Fort Sill: schools for the G.I.'s children, salons for the G.I.'s wives, a tire factory for the G.I.'s cars. Sometimes, we all get the sensation that this isn't part of the onflowing waters of human activity but a dead eddy off to the side.

Some have said (for decades now) that one day, Lawton will get better.

By dusklight, the heat loses its weight, and the cool of shadowed creeks takes the town. People sense something atavistic in all the day's illusion, and as day falls down to dark, the mirages take another form, become some throwback to a prehistoric time, some imagined realm of unfettered primality where flesh may dissolve into flesh and fists may become the leading instruments of diplomacy. Violence. Gun battles play out in the Wild Wild West of apartment complex parking lots. Fistfights and booze gatherings detail the horizon-to-horizon wilderness. In the neighborhoods where desperation is in the crumbling facades and in the child's broken bicycle upended in the yard, there are yells, then gunfire. The police sirens do not come. An ambulance. Paramedics taking their time because they know nothing is to be done here.

Some neighborhoods can fortify their boundaries against the mirages with wealth. They have community walls and hardy gardens. But though there may be gates and fences, there are no true suburbs in a rectangular town composed of four east-west thoroughfares and some number of intersecting north-south streets. And yet even with this geometrically egalitarian layout, the mirages manage to hold race to race, direct violence from cousin to cousin, and keep money among kin.

Midnight. A man needs purpose. A man finds purpose in the mirages that other men make. They head west, towards the town's most popular strip club: the Dragon West. And then, Lawton's outcasts, its perpetuators of illusion, its rough-palmed professionals, its cowboys and country boys and Goodyear toughs and west side soldiers and east side badasses and G.I.'s and marines and farmers and truckers, are all at the Dragon. And because they are the children of mirage and the abettors of mirage and the masters of mirage, they know they've come home.

2. The Dragon West

Is the only fun place in town. My mother maintains a homey atmosphere and a coterie of Korean workers but only Aryan girls as dancers, with the occasional "exotic" exception for custies to play out the fantasies of whiteness and foreign conquest, *Heart of Darkness* style.

"I want my woman to be Times New Roman in the streets and Wingdings in between the sheets," a custie told me as he gestured to the one Asian dancer we had at the time.

I retreated to the back office, where I wrote a math thesis on the properties of vortexes. I took some Ramanujan and a little bit of my Calculus textbook, and I applied some high school math to glue it all together and came up with a few not-quite-workable-but-at-least-falsifiable theorems. I was so powerfully naive that I actually believed that the math before me was some pure place where there were no nationalities, no race, no gender, and no flags.

"Who gives a fuck what they think," my mom said when I took a foolish risk and told her of my grief. "Just move on." That was the immigrant's solution to all adversity: bow your head and push fucking *harder*. Don't even allow yourself to care about others in your situation because you had *you* to take care of.

"Beside, Korean women ugly," her doorwoman told me. "That why we have to do so much."

When I disagreed, she stared at me in utter disbelief. She grew so angry she wanted to hit me. I understood. Once, my father told me I had pretty eyes. Shocked, I couldn't stop looking into a mirror for hours.

3. Lawton's seasons

December January February
Mild, with bouts of extreme, crop-killing cold

March April May
Hot

June July August
Death Hot

September October November
Hot, with tornado season

All year around, there are thunderstorms of the kind most people in the world have never experienced. Wikipedia once assured me that southwest Oklahoma, along with some peak somewhere that mountaineers fear, is the site of the most extreme weather in the world. During a typical storm, hundreds of massive, jagged bolts of lightning connect sky and earth, their glowing afterimages like light bulb filaments burning out. Thunderclaps rattle the windowpanes and sound like they're coming from beneath your feet. Seams deep within the dark earth ripping apart.

I'd underestimated love during my teenage years. I didn't know that your very cells could fall in love, to the point that their molecules get rearranged, and that this could happen without you even bothering to notice, not until you grew into a different person.

I met her in AP English. She was working on a YA novel and introduced me to capital-L Literature, which up until that point wasn't on my radar except as a means to rack up some more A's for valedictorian status. We spent lunch hours talking about *Buffy the Vampire Slayer*, and she had me over to view various other vampire movies with her girlfriends (*Blade* was tops). She asked me to the homecoming dance, and the first few times we had sex, it was nice because she had a body I couldn't stop looking at. But then there was this one time we were having sex when a hole opened up in my cranium and the sky flowed into my mind, and I realized that the top of the stratosphere must be like the bottom of the ocean, except in reverse. After we took a shower together (this was part of our routine and usually led to the next round), she stared into my eyes as she dried me off, and strange forces that move at the speed of light moved in my heart.

I broke up with her shortly after that, during one of our arguments. Except for a couple awkward, lackluster lunches here and there, we never spoke again. It was several years and a relationship later that I realized I'd been absolutely destroyed by her. The myths I'd told myself about myself were patently false. Twenty years later, and it's still terribly bad. I still wake up from dreams of her and realize that all of my cells don't understand why she isn't there beside me.

4. Lawton-Fort Sill's economy

I enjoy racist love. Being not-quite half-white makes me just minority enough for white people to feel comfortable making me their token friend, living proof that they're one of the "good ones." Being half-Korean makes them think I'm good at math and responsible, a model minority who'll contribute to society in some non-leadership, small-dick capacity. To back up these impressions, strip club money gave me nice clothes and a nice car early on, and few people would think that by age sixteen, I already knew what it was like to have to fight for my life, disarm guns, trade shots with armed robbers, and beat a large number of people into vacant-eyed expressions with my fists. Of course, people like my father, whose life was inflected with ten thousand times more violence than this, thought I was a little bitch who happened to carry around 200 pounds of muscle.

If we could turn socioeconomic makeup into geographical elevation, the plains of Lawton would become hill country with deep basins and sinkholes dotted throughout. Patterns would not obtain. Hills would cluster only occasionally. There would be a few mountains, and each of these would prove to be an eccentric solitary height, located for instance over some ramshackle ranch out in the fields. The millionaire versions of Boo Radley, redneck Great Gatsbys.

The depressions gather around undesirable locations, like near Lawton Regional Airport or along a loud thoroughfare or against the wall separating Lawton from Fort Sill, where artillery explodes continuously through the days and the nights. Many of these houses look like favela shacks, cobbled together out of castaway wood and sheets of tin. I once had to pick up a date from such a neighborhood—half-Korean happa like me—and got the address wrong twice. Both times, before I even made it to the front door, a gentleman appeared with a shotgun leveled at me and inquired after who sent me and who I was looking for and how much was owed.

Side note: the date was really into me until I took her to a Korean restaurant. Then not even the nice car could save me.

My father drove me to meet one of the town's eccentric millionaires. On the way there, he kept saying that this man was a "bigwig." When we showed up at the giant house, I noticed it had strangely cheap clapboard walls. A Rottweiler greeted us at the open front door. It shoved me aside and went out into the yard and stared off into the empty fields. The bigwig was nowhere in sight, and we just walked into the house.

The furniture looked like it had come from a club lounge. I could smell the booze and smoke on it all. A set of stairs with a walnut balustrade wound its way up to the second floor.

"Come on up," came a baritone voice. He sounded like a middle schooler who wanted his voice to be deeper than it really was.

The second floor was a bar. I mean it looked exactly like a dive bar, with booths, pool tables, and barstools, except it was part of someone's house. The bigwig was sitting with a glass of hard liquor at the longest bar I'd ever seen. He invited us over and poured us drinks. I was a teenaged teetotaler and didn't touch mine.

"Have you ever kissed a man?" he asked us.

My father explained that he had, but he hadn't realized the cross-dresser was a man.

"She" was simply beautiful, and so it wasn't his fault.

The bigwig nodded.

"It's okay to be with a man as long as you do the fucking," he explained. "If you get the fucking, you know what that makes you?"

Even the nice neighborhoods like ours couldn't aspire to grandeur. The most decadent of homes have a kind of rushed cheapness, a cutting-corners aspect to their construction. The middle-class, manicured suburban sameness that most parts of the country possess does not occur here. Lawton's homes are erected in a haphazard rush; the foundations sag, the walls crack, the roofs cave in once a strong storm passes through. An oasis, disappearing.

5. Religion in Lawton-Fort Sill

Come Sundays or even Wednesday evenings, certain churches use peer pressure especially well on teenagers. The church fathers make the kids get in a prayer circle in the center of an assembly room and surround them with a community of the already converted, many of them family and friends. Then some official will stand up with a mic and say something like:

Almighty Father in heaven…

You gave your only begotten Son for these young men and women before me. Please grant them the courage and love to accept you and join our family in Christ so that your sacrifice will not be in vain.

And help us show them the love that our Christian family holds for them. May those who've strayed from the flock find their way back. We look to them now to make the most important choice in their lives:

To accept the Lord Jesus Christ as their savior, or to continue to wander outside of the light of heaven and deny the love we all hold for them.

(Pause)

Those of you who now accept the Lord Jesus Christ into your hearts, stand up and go to the back room where members of our church family will guide you in your rebirth into a life of service.

Applause for the kids who stand and go to the back rooms, where foldout tables, donuts, and patient, kind faces awaited them.

And for those who remain:

Oh Lord, the Church on earth is but a poor reflection of your Church in heaven. Our faults may have driven away those who already belonged to you. Please forgive us for failing the young ones among us.

And may they see past our imperfections to the eternal light of your truth. I pray that we come together in worship and love so that they may one day walk the hallowed halls of your true Church in heaven.

And so on, with the official punctuating his impassioned prayer-speech every now and then with another invitation to stand and go be converted, and with more kids getting up every time. Not even I could resist by the fifth or sixth call, when the group had whittled down from fifty to just five. But I remember once—and only once—a blonde white-girl cheerleader with all the accouterments of Being Popular/one of the Plastics (low-neck shirt, heavy makeup, bubblegum chewing, light-catching jewelry, back-off facial expression, et cetera) sat surprisingly defiant through to the end, her arms crossed, her will pure iron. I never let myself underestimate her again.

When my mother convinces new girls to become strippers, she employs the same technique.

6. Stats

Lawton
Population: About 100,000
County: Comanche
Area: 80 square miles, ringed with ghost towns

Fort Sill
Population: About 53,000
Training: Army, marines.
Field trip trivia: Geronimo lived here

The Dragon West
MD educations funded: 1 (some stereotype dreams do come true)
RN/Nurse practitioner educations funded: 4
RN educations funded: 100's

7. My high school

Looked like a big, two-story cinderblock mall with windows. It had a church-style marquee, on which the guidance office put up various platitudes (*Just say no to drugs!*) and sometimes a semi-useful announcement, like "Last Day of School!" When I graduated, I drove around the school three times holding my middle finger out to it with extreme relish.

Just four more laps, and who knows? Maybe the Walls of Jericho falling.

8. Haunted locales

All teenagers in Lawton know of its haunted locations. The most famous is the parallel forest in the Wichitas. Here, an entire forest of trees grows in perfectly parallel lines, and it's not uncommon to run into a buffalo ranging through the halls of bark. Once when I was in high school, a girlfriend, her sister, and I went hiking out there. We found a pit with a decapitated armadillo laid before a hastily made wooden cross. The cross was two fencepost chunks improbably nailed together. It was moored sideways in the Indian clay, and the armadillo was draped in triangular Blair Witch Project symbols composed of three sticks each tied at their corners with twine. Its bloody head stump was alive with white maggots and iridescent green flies. My then-girlfriend took off running and fainted in the tall prairie grass, but her sister caught her, and I fanned her off and dabbed her forehead with water. She came to, clasped her hands, and said a prayer there in the swaying grasses.

The common dare is to go to those woods at night and shine your lights into its depths. You'll see the haunting sight of longshadows cast backways by the parallel trees, shadows that extend beyond the penumbra of your lights, and parallax head beams striking futilely into the gloom. Once I was out wallow-driving by myself in my teenage depression, listening to Tori Amos and telling myself I was a feminist, and I decided to take this dare. I parked behind a culvert at the mouth of the woods and turned my brights on. And staring back at me from the depths of the forest were two hugebrown human eyes full of indifference and malevolence both. The eyes approached, and I turned off the lights in panic, but this made it worse as the head floated through the black towards me. I put the car in reverse just as the decapitated head with its shaggy mane came from the trees, and as I pulled away, I saw that it was a buffalo whose body had been graded with the dark.

9. Why you cannot leave Lawton

Towards his death, my father called me and gave a long guilt-trip speech that culminated in: You need to come home and run the Dragon. I was so affronted that I said "no" harshly—"I'm not running no…." and nearly said "damn strip club." He bade me farewell.

I am a half-Asian "hick," and so I know that even more than the shotgun, our primary weapon of choice is family ties. Family ties and the associated guilt. The only way to defeat one of us "hicks" is to inflict irreparable damage upon your family, upon those ties that we use against you. Otherwise, we will win.

"Lawton is a black hole, it always sucks you back in." —Most people from my town. This is the Lawton mantra.

Shortly after I destroyed his dream of us all living in the same town again, united, my father died.

10. Prairieland Stonehenge

Many roads and streets throughout the town are flanked by tall prairie grass broken at the stems and crooked. The sight of crooked grass going on and on, the way a Stonehenge-like effect happens when the sun lines up perfectly with a long east-west street and falls burning right at its distance-diminished end, will give a man the impression of a cruel but glorious God, perhaps a barefoot God who sits in a rocking chair on His ramshackle front porch with the largest, most powerful shotgun cradled in His lap.

Many roads go by farms and ranches and fields. There are cows and horses in most of those fields, but some are empty and have no discernible purpose. Beware: rattlesnakes, copperheads, fiddlebacks, scorpions, and tarantulas of incredible variety (I once saw a delicate blue bulbous one with satanic patterns on its dangerous and beautiful body; it ran about frantically as it became a ball of fire when my father sprayed it with some flammable substance and dropped a match on it).

11. Lawton-Fort Sill artillery base

Fact: If you drive around aimlessly in Fort Sill, the MPs (military police) are guaranteed to pull you over and ask you what you're doing. You do not want this to occur.

12. Lawton's layout

Lee Boulevard West: The power lines meet at a hazy vanishing point; the squat neighborhoods are dwarfed by infinity. Here we have the Goodyear tire plant, one of the major employers alongside Fort Sill and Walmart. Growing up, most kids speak of Goodyear like East Coast kids speak of Harvard. If one isn't going into the military, this is the *non plus ultra* of our aspirations. Salaries are rumored to go as high as 60K. Slinging tires all day apparently breaks the body, and the common joke is that all your money will eventually go into back surgery.

Lee Boulevard Center: Stores will sell you special chairs for the elderly, or special cowboy attire for a rancher's needs, or special Bibles for a dear person. The wooden fences are always the same, the kind that start out sun yellow and turn the same ashgray color that all fences in Lawton eventually become.

Lee Boulevard East: No one walks the streets at night. Junk cars pile up in gravel driveways. All squalor heightened by the everglory of a sky so wide it bows into the ends of the earth, a sky sometimes streaked with long eskers and canyons of clouds, a sky whose gravid storms weep and whose stars and sun make the heart swell on some strange tide.

Gore Boulevard West: One of the barren parks has a swing set surrounded by such a desiccated vastness that no one dares go. The wind rocks the empty swings.

Gore Boulevard Center: Shopping. The neighborhoods branching off this thoroughfare have the same sign at their entrance: *Neighborhood Watch Area! Criminals Beware, Residents Watch Out For One Another!* With its dapper-hatted, Dick Tracy-like, black-ink criminal icon, the sign makes a life of crime look really cool.

Gore Boulevard East: Nice.

Cache Road West: In the fields, if you find a stick and break it, you might discover "Indian Gum" inside, a white pulpy material that we used to chew as kids.

Cache Road Center: Plaza after concrete plaza of crooked, ill-formed buildings and the same plastic-letter billboard signs, as if they were all made by the same manufacturer. Home to the Cruise, a north-south loop you're supposed to drive until you see a cute girl/guy and signal to pull over in one parking lot or another. DO NOT LOITER signs are displayed everywhere.

Cache Road East: Downtown. Once a rather lovely, historical site; now there are bad restaurants, some brick homes, and narrow roads. The yards are sliced with sidewalks people rarely use. Most of the Dragon West's employees live here, far away from work. That way they can readily tell when some creeper follows them home from the club, all the way from the town's west side, and they can have a loved one at home prepare the firearms.

Roger's Lane West: Look to the north and see the bomb smoke from the military base's guns and artillery.

Roger's Lane Center: Fort Sill's long wall runs the entire length of this thoroughfare. Some parts of it are merely razorwire fence, other parts a tall concrete wall. The earthquakes of artillery and the sound of machine-gun fire and bomb blasts are frequent and year-round.

Roger's Lane East: Trees and wilderness surround the homes. The sound of cicadas is deafening. There are mosquitoes and insects of doom. I once saw what I thought was a hummingbird in the dusk, flittering about a bush blooming with flowers. I told my father this was a good omen and snapped a picture. When the picture showed up on the camera's preview mode, I saw that the hummingbird was no bird at all, but a gigantic, horrifying moth-thing of H. P. Lovecraftian ugliness, its vermiculate horror-show bulk like some alien torso.

13. The Wichitas

To the west, north, and east of town, there stretch the Wichita Mountains, the only wrinkle in the plains landscape for many miles. They are called "mountains" perhaps out of reverence for their beauty, but most outsiders would no doubt call them hills. They are beautiful in the way very old things are beautiful, and on their slopes, the air itself feels ancient. The mountains have been weathered down by millennia and are covered in witch hazel and cacti. The boulders are called rainbow rocks because they are orange and red, and the lichen that grows on them gives them shades of pale ocean green, yellow, and even a faded velvet blue. The horizon is made of pastel colors, like a smoky rainbow laid flat against the land, and the manmade lakes go blue with the distance even if they're shitbrown up close. Vultures hang like pieces of a mobile on the sky, motionless eternally, but then you look away and look back again, and they've moved on despite their stillness.

I once found a complete buffalo skeleton behind a boulder off the side of a road. I once found a Bible beneath some rocks. I once found a fairy village made of sticks. Some child's installation? There are many strange places out there, and walking the boulder-strewn paths and trails, one thinks that if lush Appalachian forests harbor green sprightly fairies, here is a place that would give home to strange and grotesque and old fey creatures, ones with brute strength and not entirely kind eyes, though those eyes would perhaps be wise.

14. Billboards

Many of the billboards on the sides of the road are broken down, but they all have advertisements. Often, the advertisement is of a public service announcement type, but with a religious twist. One gigantic sign on the eastern edge of town that has been there my entire life reads "Jesus Saves." It depicts a sunray-emanating Christ holding his arms out to you. The icon of a savior in a vast empty plain of nothing.

LITTLE GHOST

by Danny Judge

My first impression of the abortion doctor is that he's handsome, young, and well-dressed: dressed to kill, as it were.

I can trace this equivocal need to hunt to my immediate past. It began with a doll my sister's daughter—*niece,* if I must be an *aunt*—carries always and carried two weeks ago as we gathered for Easter dinner at our mother's stucco ranch. At first glance, the doll was a toy. Then, closer: a molded embryo, scaled to size. Instead of a tiny plaything, a symbolic manifestation of the physical consequences of an emotional choice, one clearly meant for the eyes of desperate new mothers. A tiny little faceless (almost) fetus, swaddled latex in loving four-inch felt, its room temperature "flesh" used, by my own sister no less, as a little tool like phonics to teach a lesson straight and early about the insidious sin of the big goddamned A-word—to teach a *child,* a little six-year-old who strokes it lovingly with no adult sense whatsoever of its ulterior significance. Of course all this means nothing to me. I'll never choose.

I know my mind (said every loony ever). But listen: I'm pretty sure I have it pegged. I've been paying attention. More often than not, it's a cumbersome habit, the constant double-checking and stocktaking, the obsessive internal compulsion to scrape clean every corner of consciousness, no matter how grim the goop. And *this,* this sudden obsession with the doll? This is an issue of transference, this hunt I've undertaken. The eerie repose of the little "toy" embedded within me a freshly gnawing knowledge of my exclusion from "choice." I long to experience in essence the power of decision, as a woman should. *Essence.* I *need* to know there are moral stakes to physical actions; I *need* to feel danger, to mainline like an emaciated addict the molten risk to my immortal soul—to fear wrong and do it regardless, to battle the guilt my little niece's doll was molded to impart—in those that can actually muster up a fleshy doppelganger, of course... but I'm making do. I'm hunting a surrogate decision behind the cool barrel of my feminine impotence.

So I apply lip liner; I rouge my cheeks; I thicken and straighten my lashes; I dress with an audience of bare walls in my modest apartment—a temporary apartment, I'm sure. I love the color, the soft, tranquil gray. To be clear, I have the framed photos and girly hangings; I unpacked them weeks ago. But I've neglected to hang them. I look for my earrings and contemplate choice—do I choose what I wear or is he choosing for me? Do I bring my own voice or supply a conduit for the good doctor's purposeful line of clinical questioning? I love the way I run from detail by embracing it wholeheartedly. Morals and visceral id can never coexist. Truthfully? I was repulsed when I saw the thing. It is what I am, that heartburning repulsion; so far from the reaction intended, it outpaces disgust with my sister and whoever gave it to her to give to her child *et al.* Yes, my nasty little imp of an id snarled its angry teeth but simultaneously embarked upon a trail of visceral urge encroached on all sides by an overgrowth of associative stimuli, sniffing around my unconscious first, curious and then hungry, and almost immediately a perverse longing was born—the longing for consequences, for what I do with my body to matter like it does for other girls, girls who have a stake in the little blue-swaddled doll, who feel the disgust of its implications in their fecund uteri.

Ugh. And my teachers said I was too smart for my own good. Well, the teachers with children said I overthought things... too analytical, they cried, their mouths full of sticky caramel fertility... the old childless cat ladies loved me. Bad omen. Hope their cats were tabbies...omens enough: too smart... right... fuck karmic cats *I don't own one* if I did, however, (fuck karma, that is), I wouldn't have to fuss with PlannedP or PlanB—I *would* make him wrap it: karma plays dirty, no telling where he's been... no baby worries though *what's the Marley song?* "No Egg No Cry?" No... no "*Woman*"... ah, but to me, for me, me... interchangeable, aren't they?

What do I wear? How do I talk? So different from a typical date. How do I make sure he wants more, that he doesn't say goodnight and run? I can't choose if he wants no part of me. Then, the choice: *Can I, Will I?* And oh god if I do (if I *choose* to before the night ends) let it not be a rebellion against heart and mind, lest I lose myself to this pervasive little imp. Let it be because I want it. Let it be a mistake made in the heat of wanton dereliction.

How to start: Do we shake hands or hug like old friends? Why have I hung nothing in here, unpacked every box but hung nothing? Is a skirt appropriate? I remind myself again *This is My choice My body My life* and the doctor knocks on time.

His handwriting, for chrissakes, must be perfect.

My junkie heart gasps, arches its bloody back off the stained silk sheets of my barren chest cavity as an adrenaline rush purges my blood of doubt—I make a choice but it's too late and far too rude to call it off now, and the id is laughing. She holds my leash, for now. The doctor's arrival, at the very least, punctuates the mounting inanity of my thoughts. No use reaching for it now—*where was I? why am I doing this?* Distracted, blissfully occupied. The impish id retreats while I appraise him, silent until I'm comfortable enough to look ahead.

He's supposed to be this evil baby-killer, an evil effigy of a man with rubber gloves and glass eyes, but on my doorstep he's a nice young man, my age. He's slicked his hair back and sidelong ala Dean Martin—a classic, tone-deaf but pragmatic sense of style that somehow means he is free of tattoos, piercings and frivolity, that he sips wine socially, knows where to grasp the glass without knowing the year by smell or bouquet, or even what "bouquet" means. Even worse (because it relaxes me and draws me closer before a word is spoken), he looks as nervous as I feel.

"Hi. Rachel?"

And so the night becomes an exercise in redolent discovery.

Without flashing all the way back I can trace myself, my present predicament, if not *me-myself* in the Whitmanian sense, to a Saturday in September eleven years ago in the foyer of my mother and father's stucco ranch, to my bold introduction of a nervous, half-Jewish, half-black boy from a neighboring school to my Methodist parents, who practically asphyxiated themselves in a fit of white restraint. I can step far enough back to the shameful satisfaction I gleaned from their discomfort and no further. I've forgotten Allen's face. Alec? Alvin? Of course, I remember the looks on theirs with photographic clarity, and why that should be and who, if anyone, should shoulder the blame, if not me, is an

issue for the dream journal I keep by my bed for this exact purpose—to unburden my conscious conscience of sleepy relics of the buried other.

Though I've never hunted, I imagine the adrenal cocktail that first time out must feel like this: a slow emotional descent into vigilant patience, leading to a keener taste of the wind and a sharpening awareness: the focus needed to track little side-swept twigs, all the while suspecting deep down that the biggest rush is lurking close by or just ahead, your glands ready to thrust you into manic slow-motion at the slightest provocation. I suppose out of necessity they tape their… well, "themselves" down to dispel the discomfort of the unceasing erection that this state of pure expectation must inevitably breed, for how else can they manage the excruciating tightness of that imminent, incendiary, inevitable *choice*—pull the trigger or let him go? My father was a hunter before he died, and the stucco ranch became my mother's empty box—*goddamn,* my dream journal is underqualified.

And all I want is to be a woman: all I want is to make a mistake with this man that involves sex. Simple transference. I'm not all that complex, am I? I'm not a Judy Bloom character. I'm not *that* fucked up—looking at you, Margaret.

So like the tree-born hunter I tuck away my tension and observe the details informing my imminent choice: his pupils like flecked pollen, here and for an instant fluttering there; his Adam's apple bedded by a subtle, V-shaped slope of white cotton where his cornflower blue tie unites his firm collar, the cartilage unobtrusively proportionate within a network of flesh-eclipsed muscle; his confident yet deferential bearing and the fine hair on the back of his hands, thin enough, thick enough; and I know he's waiting as well, watching and listening, apprais-ing me with his clinical eye, perhaps the slope of my breasts or evocative bitten lip I affect quite shame-lessly, knowing full well what I've done.

In the interest of deferring with optimism to what I already recognize as an embryonic phys-ical attraction, I think only fleetingly of the details missing from the latex form of my niece's toy ghost, hold their absence only for an instant against the tapestry of his thirty years of fine tuning, and even now I do this reflexively, for I've aged thirteen Acura turns since I feared my dubious id and the portent of my juvenile rebellion and, already, for better or worse, I detect a human element beneath the veil of cognitive murk that polluted my expectations. With the land so sprawling, what can the hunter do but document what proximity demands he must, if for no other reason than to retain the holy illusion of agency—and, of course, suppress the tightly wound imp that lurks still, because the id never recuses herself. Six lefts and seven rights, tracking my path through a forest of latent chaos, because, simply put, I see myself fucking the doctor, so checking his speed and the suspicious loiterer shrinking in the side-view mirror keeps me aware, keeps me di-vorced from my seesawing whims.

I slow this vehicle down and he slows his. I act like a lady, and he acts like my date, not my doctor, which is great because he isn't. Won't be. I just have no need for him in that capacity, which, ironically, is why we're here together. The restaurant is nice; nevertheless, the rich are procreators too—a child named Cody That's Enough! in the booth be-hind us, unseen and never to be seen. He screams bloody shards of glass that tear jagged holes in the heavenly sheen of our public isolation, and not for an instant does the child recall the doll. His pocket square accessorizes his low-key sense of style, and not even then do I connect the silky, virile blue with the four-by-four swaddle that houses my niece's tac-tically poignant little latex companion. Later I see it, long after the beast leaps sprinting full throttle from the brush into the great wide open and, as it always does, disappoints at the moment of climax—*should I have waited? Just to see how I felt tomorrow?*

He tells me things a human tells anoth-er human: his grandmother raised him after the death of his parents, the tragic death he mentions only when I press back in time from his nobly un-dertaken vocational calling. I probe, prod and feel around the id's clumsy hunger to know and expose: *why* do you… *how* does one even… Because that's part of the choice, not knowing, wanting to know, not *knowing* why I *have* to know and knowing that finding out would ruin everything—

"What do you like to do?" he asks, inter-rupting the movie I'd been watching, the epic story of us in this place, this ridiculous place.

"I knit."

I don't fucking *knit.* Why—

"What do you knit?" He feigns interest above a glistening trickle of duck sauce, rogue and wild against the clean white porcelain of his six-ty-dollar plate.

"Little blue blankets. For babies."

Jesus. At this point, I'm just along for the ride. My innocence is on autopilot.

"Oh?"

I wouldn't know what to say to me, either.

Later, at home, a half-hour after I've chosen.

Without turning on my bedroom light, I remove my earrings, my clothes, my lipstick, and, though I cannot see them, I nevertheless feel the vacuum of my unadorned walls. I can almost hear my ambivalent independence echoing unchecked and purposeless from the clean corners. I slip naked between my blue cotton sheet and my heavy comforter. Soon the satisfied little imp vanishes beneath the thin membrane that separates the deep from my unsatisfied mind.

Put the damn pictures up, I think.

Okay, I think.

THE TRIALS OF TOBIT

by Joseph Lisowski

DIVISION/PRELUDE

I am Tobit.
My father is called "God is Good,"
my grandfather, "God is Merciful."
How can I not be blessed?

I have a story, even a song—it rises
like evening smoke—the crackle
of roasted lamb turning on the spit—gentle
wind, a ticking of grains of sand
brushing cheek, forehead, tip of tongue.

My story, of course, is of family—
Of how I do and do not belong.

ORIGINS

When my father died,
he left me an orphan.
I offered first fruits,
first shearings of my sheep,
firstlings of my flock
to no avail.
The priests took my tithes,
drank my wine, ate
my figs, pomegranates—my
brothers ate the food of heathens.
I reaped the wind.

Changes occurred. I married.
Roads became unsafe.
A new king flogged
the desert, overturning stones—
the dead had no place to rest.
I listened long to their conversations.
And then girded my loins.

EXCESS

Everywhere I turn the dead lay.
a feast for insects, vermin,
some ignored, stiff as leather.
I return at night, shovel in hand,
wildly displace sand.
The bodies sink to a level of light
becoming dark, night.
Enough of a crypt for passage.

The king hears of my treachery,
clangs the death-knell,
begins confiscating my land, furniture, food,
servants, clothes, precious gems, all
but my wife and son.
I flee on a manna wind
where locusts are sweet, plenty.

The king dies at the hands of his sons,
who now scour the desert,
looking for me
seeking solace from one
whose father has died.

LEGACY

Patricides are forever lost.
A new king reigns—I'm
welcomed back, reunited
with wife and son.

At the feast of weeks,
fifty days from Passover,
I am feted with sweetest meats,
wine, bread, fruits.
I send my son to find a poor man,
someone to share our wealth.
He returns alarmed—"Father, one
of our people has been murdered.
He lies in the marketplace
where he had been strangled."

I rush out, gather the body,

take him home, to my room
to wait for night and burial.
I wash and with sadness return to
the empty banquet hall.
I think of the prophet Amos, widely heralded
As the prophet of love who said,
"Your festivals shall be turned into mourning
and all your songs into lamentation."

My son is gone.
I weep. At sunset, I will go out
and dig a grave, bury my guest.

SLEEP OF THE JUST

"What is wrong with you!" my neighbors
complain. "For this, you were hunted down,
almost executed. For this you escaped?
To bury the dead again?"

It is hot. I am tired.
What is done is done.
I doze, my face uncovered.

I wake easy from a sleep of the just,
my eyes heavy, I think, with sand.
No, my wife says. Bird droppings have
Filled my eyes. She takes me
to doctors. Their salves
seal my vision. My kinsmen
stay a while, but then none remain.

My wife goes out looking for work.

WOMAN'S WORK

My wife weaves, "the kind of work
women do." The owners
are always pleased; they pay
well, more than feels right.

One night she brings
a young goat back with her.
"Return this," I demand. "Why

are you now a thief!"
"A bonus, a bonus!" she insists.

A bone, a bone is what I hear.
And with this I must contend.
"See, Your true character
is finally showing itself!" she screams.

LIKE A PEACOCK

I hate this life,
the parts I play,
now begging God
with praise to do my bidding,
to take away my life
or the insults of others.

How dumb do I think he is?
my sincerity sweet
As undigested cud.
How dumb does he think
I am to pray so transparently?

When I lost sight,
I lost vision. Courage, too.
Shamelessly, I preen
like a peacock, flaunting
my humility.

THE FOLLY OF PRIVILEGE

I am a rich man,
treasured in another country.
I have hidden wealth
that my son must retrieve.

He must hire a guide—his spirit
is young, judgment not quite
of a piece—a man tested, unbroken,
a true kinsman, loyal friend
to love not money.
Who but an angel?

It must be "God who heals."

GOOD FORTUNE

Raphael broods like high mountain fire,
licks grass, sticks, embers to rise
merely a tenth of an inch,
the precise distance between heaven and earth.
Barely enough to ignite imagination.

He agrees to serve Tobiah, luckless son
Of a blind prophet born of shadows, snakes.

AS LUCK WOULD HAVE IT

A boy and his dog leave home,
Followed by the angel.
The travelers walk until nightfall
and make camp at the Tigris River
where the boy washes his feet.

A large fish suddenly leaps
from the water, tries to swallow his foot.
The angel tells him to seize the fish,
which he does and hauls upon shore.
"Cut the fish open and take out
its gall, heart, and liver. Keep them
with you but throw away the entrails."

The boy does as bid. "But why?" he asks.
"Burn heart and liver—its smoke purges any demons
nearby, banishes them forever. Gall, when rubbed
on the eyes of a man with cataracts, restores sight.
Believe and obey. Trust and obey."

And the boy, nothing but his father's son, obeys.

A MATTER OF HOPE

The boy marries a girl
and her secrets, which
he only partially understands.
First marriages are always
a matter of hope.

Hers is a lovely story,
left for another time.

UNKNOWN HEART-ACHE

It's a dream world,
fancy fed, love directed,
if the boy charmed, blessed,
follows good advice, respects
elders and angels.

It is easy for him to obey.
Great wealth, ease is promised.
He is not tempted to turn away.
Darkness has no appeal.
Death holds no beguiling veil,
which he is driven to lift.

And women are nothing to fear.

AT END, A BEGINNING

He enters her arms
And does not die.
Earlier, he prepared a spell
to cast out her death demon.
His life in balance, no tremors,
no fears, he believes himself safe.
And so he is.

A boy who lives by faith
or one that gives little thought?
Perhaps he is the son
as imagined by the father—
easy, ready, unable to break.

THE OLD MAN
(*Excerpt from* Deep-Rooted Cane)
by Sarah T.

Author's note: The novel excerpted below is a pastiche of Jean Toomer's (1923) "Cane", which was set in the rural Southern community in which the landowners' small cane fields were the setting for all manners of drama and passion and human interaction. My re-telling of "Cane" resurrects, among other things, Toomer's many characters who died in the cane and gives life to one very minor but compelling character most frequently referred to as "the Old Man". Readers know little of the old man other than what the other characters project onto him during about a dozen conjectures about his life throughout the course of the book. All we really know of the Old Man is that he sits in the corner of the basement of a wheelwright's shop, and that he is fed by a little girl. He speaks just once, giving a brief but eloquent pronouncement of guilt on the area's plantation elite. He is described as being deaf and blind and immobile, but I don't know about that last part. He captivated me, and I came to believe in his mobility. I hope you enjoy the way I put him in motion.

> "Oracular.
> Redolent of fermenting syrup.
> Purple of the dusk.
> Deep-rooted cane."
> - Toomer, 1923

"He is like a bust in black walnut. Gray-bearded. Gray haired. Immobile. ... The only word he says is sin." —Jean Toomer

Barlo stood back, knowing that the old man, for the moment, was off again in spirit. He leaned in and tied a blue satin scarf around his neck. He could see that the old man's face was serene.

The old man, the *houngan,* was out of his body, free from its humiliations and constraints, flying above the pine and assessing the crossroads, the cotton, and the cane. The town stood small but erect in the midst of the pastoral calm. All was as it usually was at dusk. Deer lay down on soft needles along the pine forest's edge, or sniffed the wind and ambled along the line of trees. A family of warblers nested in a tree nearby, and a blackbird took to flight from the forest across from the Limons' break of cane.

Mame Lamkin's husband had wandered out to the forest's edge past the animals. The year that had passed between his murder and the moment of the old man's flight had not seemed to change him at all save for the wispy thinness of a dead-self in limbo that had replaced the manly flesh in which he had once lived. He swayed against the wind current, looking down on his mangled midsection in agonized translucence. His eyes hung down, no longer looking for the vigilantes who had dismembered him, nor his lily-White lover who had sat in her house and chewed her nails—tellingly—while the buzzards plucked at the Black flesh to which she'd once clung. He sensed the old man, and lifted his empty, invisible eye sockets to the moon. The old man moved beyond the ghost and his sorrow.

At the crossroads, the old man saw Becky, ethereally unearthed from the rubble of her cabin, waiting for her sons to come home. He saw Bob Stone holding his neck as if he wanted to stop the blood, though the blood had stopped running many months ago, hours after Tom Burwell's blade had slid across it in Bob's own patch of cane. Bob and Becky—these prematurely dead in their individual levels of limbo—hovered nearly on top of each other. But neither of them knew that the other was there. They swayed and searched and wondered, only somewhat aware that they existed in a space from which they could neither escape nor return to their lives. A long-tailed weasel burrowed in the earth underneath them.

Too many sorrowful spirits and too much

unjust blood hung around the fields and forests of Sempter. When he flew too low, too close to it all, the disembodied old man choked with sorrow, like the fist that is the past will do to a man, and brought the days before the end of slavery up from his core. His memories of the sugar mill and the bell rack and the scent of cane syrup mixed with burnt human flesh were threatening to pull him down, so he lifted high up above it, to the line of tree tops that only the black birds could see. He made a swift but thorough pass through the fields of the Limon family; their land extended as far as the old man could see, over hills and into valleys, beyond the beyond and back.

From the distance at which the old man flew, the earth appeared to be perfect. It was green. Breezy. Free from its history and its reality, the earth was the picture of peace. Besides the stranded spirits and the scattered animals, no one was nearby. Behind him were the pine trees, the road that edged along them, and the wheelwright's workshop where the ceremony to feed and honor the obviously angry *loa* would go on.

Off to the old man's side just beyond the limit of his vision was the compound begun by his Barlo, which the old man knew he may not even live to see completed. But that didn't matter much to him anyway. The compound was Barlo's project. His was simply getting through this life.

In front of the flying old man was acre upon acre of land, reminding him of time and the place that he'd grown from infancy and slavery into freedom and manhood. He turned and sent himself down the hill toward his right. He passed a bobcat on a rock and came to the Sempter crossroads. To its left was a cluster of Creek family homes—a small community that the Negroes aptly called *The Left-Overs*. A "half-breed" moved down the road toward the door of one of The Left-Overs' homes. The half-breed flinched as though he wanted to acknowledge the old man, but instead covered his head and kept moving. The old man free-fell down the air some to see the man, but stayed a respectful distance away and kept on going his own way. He careened above some sleeping geese in the rotting tree swamp, then turned and emerged in the midst of the cluster of shanties beyond.

The guard of the Negro quarters, whom they no longer called the *overseer*, oversaw the activities of the cluster of shanties from his raised brick one-room wood house with the rickety porch.

"That forehead. Great wooly beard. Those eyes. A mute John the Baptist of a new religion—a tongue-tied shadow of an old."

- Toomer, 1923

He sat there with the lamp on, and he listened. The Negro yards were empty and quiet, and most of its lamp lights were out. The old man knew that the sheriff had told the guard to keep the Black folk in tonight, so the old man passed the shanties and the shack of the guard as well. He couldn't stand the scent of the blood on that man's hands, and so he stayed away from it and thus away from his own rage. He engaged himself in the mission of his flight.

> "For though the sun is setting on
> A song-lit race of slaves, it has not set;
> Though late, O soil, it is not too late yet
> To catch thy plaintive soul, leaving, soon gone,
> Leaving, to catch thy plaintive soul soon gone."
> - Toomer, 1923

He saw the Sempter chapel, but knew he couldn't get close. It wasn't the column of buzzards that kept him away, but the impenetrable protection all around the building that would bounce the man off like a ball. He came across the quarters to the front Big House instead. The audacious antebellum mansion glowed in the red moonlight and appeared to him as a pinkish familiar place. It welcomed him weirdly toward its insides. The magnolias had just begun to bloom, so he allowed their scent to guide him toward the mansion's iron gate. He saw its sign, down in front, and knew, from years of working there for free and then for pocket change on the dollar, that the name of the place was painted on the sign's face. *Tempus Plantandi*, it said—what the Limon family called their old family home.

Each of the second floor windows above the pillared porch of Plantandi was open just a bit, and he chose the one just to the right of center to go through into the house. Once in, he found the mistress, Young Dave's wife, unmoving, anesthetized from those of Barlo's herbs Old Chromo had cooked into her cobbler. Ol' Massa Dave's wife, the withered Mistress Limon, slept stone still in her ancient Victorian bedclothes and four-poster Victorian bed in the master bedroom down the stately hall. A servant reclined in a rocking chair in the corner of the room, sleeping lightly and dreaming of 4 different-colored horses. She whispered something and clasped the cross that hung around her neck as the old man passed in spirit and kept on going.

There were vases and chaises and mirrors and bureaus and carpets and cupboards and dishes and silver and doilies and curtains and covers and photos and paintings and gadgets and statues and more of the trappings of particularity and excessive wealth within the mansion around him. The stretched, framed, and hung needlepoint on the wall read, in fancy script, "Reap the harvest of your land. —*Leviticus.*" But the old man couldn't read it. His eyes were back in body, they were blind anyhow, and had never beheld the grammar books and readers the Big House children sat on the porch and read. He swept right past the cross-stitched directive and the myriad heirlooms, pleased with how disinterested he was in the meaningless items that mattered so much to this upright old family. He had coveted their stuff in slavery days when he was young himself. But none of it seemed to matter at this moment. He was freer than emancipated. He had no use for anything, nothing but the fresh food that the girl from the Big House brought him, the rhythm of the drums, his tall wooden staff from the Motherland, the rattle of the *ascon*, and the prayer chants of his godson and flight and dreams and Mother Africa—his homeland, his *'Nan Ginee*—where he would surely go as soon as his worn-out body gave up on him and released him once and for all. Soon his body wouldn't matter, and heirlooms and items would be worthless things of the past.

> "'Sin...Th sin whats fixed...upon th white folks...f tellin Jesus lies. O th sin th white folks 'mitted when they made th Bible lie.' ...The old man sinks back into his stony silence."
> - Toomer, 1923

"Time and space have no meaning in a canefield.
No more than the interminable stalks."
- Toomer, 1923

LIKE MANY GIANT FOOTPRINTS

by William Doreski

You claim that despair stalks friends,
poaching in their teacups and slurring
their favorite words. The cold wind
tastes of stone. The post office
slumps on its foundations. Mail
from the last century still awaits
delivery, gummed flaps muttering.
Meanwhile the wind plunges and plunges
with the angst of dolphins hunted
to extinction. Shoppers toting bags

of primary goods recall
their childhoods in other nations,
even if born here in a welter
of sticky limbs. You want to warn them
that when the snowdrifts melt
certain clues will emerge. Maybe
diamond tiaras stolen too late
to catch the evening news. Maybe
cigar butts that crawled from Cuba
to subvert fat-headed old men

who always vote Republican.
The newly kindled sunlight fails
to deter the wind from prying
into our open pores and scalding
tears we've saved for our funerals.
But you laugh your rhinestone laugh
and note that wherever volcanoes
burst the earth new opportunities
follow, like many giant footprints
leading to the planet's far edge.

CLAY-COLORED

by William Doreski

Miranda steals shiny trinkets
from the elderly and pawns them.
When I reach into her bosom

and extract my Timex watch
her innocence recedes like a tide.
A crowd gathers. Miranda

in a pique of fury undresses
completely, shedding jewelry,
pill boxes, lighters, money clips,

and enough watches to daunt
every time zone on the planet.
Naked, she glowers with fission.

Her jaws creak as if a great scream
has fossilized deep inside her.
The crowd murmurs with pity

and glowers at me, so I leave
with my watch ticking on my wrist
and a vision of Miranda's

clay-colored body brimming.
The rest of the day discolors
like an old bruise. The post office

coughs up bills and circulars.
The coffee shop's too busy
to prepare my mocha latte

with the right shade of chocolate.
The market offers weird cuts of beef
crudely torn from celestial cows.

Miranda will probably stalk
and knife me in my sleep;

and when police find my watch

ticking in her bosom she'll feign
such guilt they'll feel ashamed,
and neglect to arrest her.

BROOKLYN FERRY, A GHOST STORY

by William Doreski

After taking my daily pills
I fall from the ferry and drown.
The Brooklyn Ferry, Whitman's beard

plowing the river in sparkles
of sun. The engine smuts
the yellow sky with coal smoke.

The passengers in smelly woolens
clump like clots of moss on rock.
Manhattan without skyscrapers

exudes a rattle of carts, drays,
and wagons. Whitman tosses
a life preserver to save me,

but I'm so old and stony I sink
with pitiless glee to the bottom.
The mud engorges me. I'm fish

food before I've finished drowning.
This isn't funny, but the crowd
on the ferry laughs a huge gray

nineteenth century laugh designed
to drive its victims insane.
I can hear it while the fish nose

and nibble and my lungs pump
like sump pumps and the fresh
but oily water mingles with salt

to brew my future in the stars.
The Brooklyn Ferry hasn't run
since John and Washington Roebling

completed their gothic bridge
with diagonal harp-strung cables

and walkway down the center.

I'm walking that walkway right now.
I wave at the crowd of ghosts
on the ghost ferry steaming across

the East River with coal smoke
the color of Whitman's beard
and a school of grim suicides

paddling in its wake, every one
determined to reach Manhattan
before it finally drifts away.

THE LOBOTOMIZING ANGEL

by William Doreski

My journals shredded overnight,
refuting every hard-earned word.
The computer's cyclops eye self
blinded, erasing the only
locally competitive intellect.
Shelves of books have toppled.

When I paw through their pages
each is blank. War and politics
flashed and thundered after midnight.
Yet the scribbles in my journals
and the text painfully typed
into my computer said nothing

about healing the rasp of bone
on bone, metal on bedrock.
I didn't name names except those
Adam refused to whisper to Eve.
But the lobotomizing angel
has flitted through my house

to deny my lifetime of work
a hearing. I sweep up the scraps
of journal and toss the junk
computer into a trash bag
for a trip to the landfill. Maybe
after a while the text will return

to those formerly printed books.
Snowdrifts thaw slowly in weak
March sun. The longest month
of the year. Or so I scrawled
in one of those vandalized journals,
or maybe typed on the laptop

that no longer possesses a mind.
Self-rebuttal's out of fashion—

nuclear war glooms the horizon,
and the chat of birds at the feeders
effects a grammar too vivid
for any journal to contain.

FROM BARTLETT'S QUOTATIONS

by William Doreski

Reading from *Bartlett's Quotations*
aloud in the coffee shop
you smother all conversations

and frustrate people on cell phones
chatting about private matters
they wish to expose to the world.

"A stitch in time saves nothing,"
you read. "A fool and his bladder
are soon parted." "Early to bed,

better off dead." "Red sky at dusk,
your sailboat will rust." Which edition
of Bartlett's are you quoting?

Your expression clouds. Customers
shrug into their coats and depart.
The coffee smells of formaldehyde.

Far beneath us a volcano
is brewing, its evil temper
a dream of molten crystals.

Long after we're gone it will surge
like a boil and pop. The lava
will erase this civilization

and cool into layers of basalt
too black to let warmth or light escape
to encourage new evolutions.

Only your ghost will linger,
mouthing new crops of quotations
but no longer sounding them.

At last you close your book and stare
into your coffee cup, exhausted

by scholarly exertion. I snatch

the book and flip through it.
Every page is blank. Outside,
a snow shower blinds the parking lot

with a dense gray scrim, and silence
maps its heavy old footfall
from here to there and back again.

DEVIL IN A BLUE DRESS

by Nancy Flynn

She's blue
the I that turned into this
you.   This I, an I-
oh, you.
Easier to ad
-dress, to dis/appear
in a dress.
            Simpler
to split the atom
-ized or (even) the atomizer of your/my
choice perfume.
            You, on the other
hand, back
-ward leaning, lured
memories, stick your
tongue out—who has the upper
hand?   Hear.

*

            Here.
                        Your eyes
used to be blue. Envied, shift
to green. The crystal gaze would say
impure. The bluest *ai*
yi yi, do stet away—
the Is   the yous
the eyes   the ewes
the poet Ai   the use.

*

I
am speaking to
the you,
the one I ceded my
lost/last voice,
I—

better entrusted to you?

You with that loveliest
oo & leading, yielding
Y. Of the why versus
I don't like the way a mouth must
shape, grimace
the I, more *ai yi yi*

this I
this I used
this I used to want,
crave see,
be seen—the eye beheld,
others who'd cast the
eye you/I, me
up.

But now I've turned to
you, historic
you who used to
do/be that,
a cardboard cut,
scissors in a
hand.

No more the I, the in & out
a door, that skeleton key,
the glassed-in porch.
Where you sat.
Where I watched.
Where we cleaved to split.
Where we shed, we
left, two
skins. Excused from
chatter, blast/bombast.
The tried & trying,
true. Tired now?
It's true.

*

I have been teaching myself to want.
You have been wondering if it would stick.
The riddle outside her
        blind, my blinds, your bind, the long
        un/winding road.

A self that's split & I who eyes about
the world, first person claimed but (still) thinking you.
You that's the eye
seen third and, I
who wisely took the seat in
back, set out to watch
this reconnoitered
you, that you who did it—
risky
stumbling
fell.

Her solo path.
Yours, too. The wringing out of
words   do ring, mere
hands   do script & fail
me
too & erase
you.

*

The bluest eye
The bluest I
The bluest you who blew
in blustery & blessed,
a blister on the bruise that's you,
my shins, her high high
shoes.

The eye/I is an unreliable, an
oracle, the I is a
dunce & a stumble, a
butcher baker candlestick
maker, rapscallion thief. The I is a pole with
hat & shoes. You, oh you, the you is a
woo. The ewe is a world in curled-right wool.

Life is a short eye/short   I
blink.
For O, she's
blue the I that's
turned,
turned into this: this,
you.

BRASS TYRANT AND THE AMERICAN THIRST

(Excerpt from Feverglades*)*

by Kirk Marshall

Whiskey had never fascinated or enthralled him. When Briggs was much younger, when his tastebuds were sharper and his craving for liquid sanctuary not yet implicated by years of professional intervention and support group therapy, he had found the attraction of whiskey as a preferred victual to be a muted one. Briggs had been a beer drinker, perhaps unimaginatively so, or else he had gravitated towards Caribbean-branded rum, because the fuzzy logic of exoticism had held sway for him over the provincial timidity of homegrown imports. For him, American-distilled whiskey was a libation for an earlier mindset, one enamoured of history: those good ole' boys whom fawned and deliquesced over their Kentucky straight did not drink to forget; they drank to remember. For Briggs, they were revivalists of a scattered confederacy, a grey covenant which decreed that drunkenness was the province of history. Briggs wouldn't have been surprised to one day encounter a thousand thousand silver liars all assembled at the bar teak, conveyed in their Civil War Union sack coats, their pillbox caps, their brass buttons, riding boots, russet-coloured brogans, their gold-fringed epaulettes, their blood-spattered faces, their soot-whitened whiskers, their saber-scarred cheekbones. Sometimes he would come across a bald-pated ancient nursing a dram of whiskey, cupping his ear to the glass as if harkening through the centuries to the acrid rumble of cannon fire. Sometimes he would catch a wrinkle-sunken sentimentalist inhaling from his whiskey snifter as if responding to sulphur notes of cordite and decay. Some days Briggs would observe the whiskey-blinded hobos on the New Jersey streets, those rag-and-bone men hobbled by uncoordinated thirsts who tussled for change while clutching brown paper bags like Chinese lanterns before them, and he would think the drink was a cruel inheritance, like a nation-building bullet once lodged in the spleen during the heat of the fray and slowly disintegrating. Whiskey only ever seemed to eat away at a person's insides while the host deluded himself that it was the stuff of ceremony, of romance and Reconstruction. But it was closer to an autoimmune infection exclusive to American dynasties, Briggs reasoned, a thing which southern sons learned at the bottom of their daddy's bottle.

Briggs wouldn't have been convinced otherwise—would never have revised his soft loathing for the drink, or his once-adversarial disenchantment over displays of public sentiment—if not for one evening in which whiskey was redefined for him as a language he'd heretofore failed to discern. And not just any language, but a language of control. He had been twenty-five years old at the time, had temporarily relocated from Elizabeth, New Jersey, to the industrial exurbs of south-central Brooklyn only a gloaming of months prior, and had temporarily hustled his way into an imitation of liquidity, had wiled his way into a gig tending bar at an oak-staked hole-in-the-wall taproom called The Brass Tyrant. The place had proven popular among a certain set of men sporting dark complexions and distressing dentistry, and it was storied as a living relic of Gravesend: a *nouveau-riche* salon for piss-soaked libertines of a not wholly-fabricated standing; a chink in the pectoral of Cronos, where past intrigues had not yet been buffed by the sculpting of Time. It seemed anyone who frequented the Tyrant had a story, and not a negligible few threatened finding the facts to support them.

There were patrons who were all-day drinkers, mouthy old hellraisers baffled by loss or cirrhosis of the liver, they who would lounge against the banquettes of red leather like macaques in thermal waters. There were droll salt-eyed dockworkers who hunkered in a low mutter over the green baize of their wall-flocked tables like croupiers sharing a midnight cigarette between shifts. There were queer one-dollar Johnnies in zoot suits, overalls, jailbird castoffs, brickmakers' knickerbocker breeches, who cashed their welfare cheques for another week delaying the making good of their egregious tabs.

Amongst them sat veterans of at least three different wars, all graced with the look of souls wracked by *saudade*, an ache for a country to which they no longer belonged. There were aged black jazz romantics, galvanic pop-eyed journalists of New York's symphonic frontier who now piloted taxis, serviced hotel washrooms, manned sidewalk crêperies, but who spoke of the maligned legacy of the clarinet in the bebop grooves of Duke Ellington, of joints in N'Orleans that still shivered with energy like lizards in spring. They would stake each jug of suds on a game of *morra*, would strike their hands against the luminous felt surface of their booth, would giggle wildly and purse their faces into an *embouchure* while sampling sweet *horchata* ale through moustaches of foam. There were one or two hipsters donning beards and beanies, pink-faced and blinking from their perches along the bar as they wrestled with assigned texts, clamoured over MFA coursework or ethical clearance collateral. A resident playwright would sometimes commandeer a table in the back, endure an hour hissing into a dictaphone, before evacuating his post to slink out into the rude Brooklyn winter. There were days when Briggs could just watch them all, this curious misbegotten clientele, and recognise them for what they were: folks in search of a haunt where they could be alone together, and therefore a little less alone.

The infrequent female patrons whom The Brass Tyrant might regard as its demimonde were few and far between, and Briggs likened them to day-pass visitors of prison inmates insofar that they were afforded access to even the most coveted tables reserved for regulars, could stalk the red oak floorboards with their baskets selling roses or their fresh-laundered housedresses in storage bags hoisted over their shoulders, and in minutes they were in orbit again, had tossed back a Manhattan or Pisco Sour or Perrier, before all assuming a compelling exit, a volley of feminine softness for the downwind lake-effect snow to swallow. They were like visitors, Briggs noticed, because when they left, there was a finality in their vanishing; one could not account for their return, and tomorrow would be as though such business, a freedom available in the sweetness of female company, was only rumour, not even that. Oftentimes it made him think of his sister, but this just excelled in aggravating his feelings of isolation and solastalgia, and he was certain it was harder on her end, so much harder, and he would short-circuit the shame by refusing to succumb to sentiment. He would merely watch the girls, and admire their vitality.

After a few weeks of familiarisation and suspected workplace hazing, Briggs began to notice that a small cadre of the cattier girls, with their smirking eyes and their wry delight in writhing confrontation—which were the ones he favoured, every one of them looking like a black-haired gypsy visitation, as if augured under the star of Lorraine Bracco or Catherine Zeta-Jones—would collaborate to spurn and needle the old geezers clustered at the bar, would whisper mocking invitations into their gnarled grey skulls, would simper and flash their teeth at the wheezy bench liars in a dance of intimacy and menace. If the day was a slow one, and the customers indifferent to his attention, Briggs learned to train his eyes on that coven of old geezers converged at the rear of the bar. The girls feigned to compete for their attention, but the wheezy bench liars remained unmoved. It was then that Briggs came to realise that the girls were *performing* their false flirtations, but not as he had first intuited; that is to say, the girls were pretending to bait the geezers not because of the thrill of the taunt, but because they genuinely wanted to seduce the ancients with their cobbled flesh.

He convinced himself that it was the geezers who were taunting the girls: their power resulted not from resistance, but from systematic disinterest. The longer he lingered in The Brass Tyrant, the less transfixed he was by the women and the more vested he became in verifying the allure of the old liars, in gaining their approval and so inheriting their secrets. They each possessed the whittled oblique face of a church fresco icon, a chalk-white bust like a Hans Holbein cameo clamped in a locket. Yet assembled together, they resembled an Early Flemish panel-portrait executed by the Brothers van Eyk, the Ghent Altarpiece of Time-eaten Gremlins. Their rickety pisshead clan behaved in such a way that Briggs was often privately reminded of the Muppets in the mezzanine, as if Statler and Waldorf had emerged with raspy scorn from the television set to crack wise about the state of his life. He didn't need anyone to explain to him that these men were gangsters, the fathers of criminal progeny. Briggs was old enough to deduce that you didn't earn a living by drinking: each of these geezers fraternised this humid oak taproom not to toast past triumphs, but to conduct their business. When the girls nuzzled close, they weren't auditioning attempts at arousal but being whispered *to*; when the girls departed, they weren't leaving to pursue suckers beyond the bar's periphery, but doing as instructed, inheriting the dirty work of the geezers who would sit, wait, and forecast their gambles. These weren't men who congregated to reminisce, Briggs saw. These were men who strategised to determine a virgin future.

And these men drank whiskey. It would've been reductive or conflative or uninterrogative of him to assert that it was the drink that endowed the men with their power, but as Briggs was the one frequently called on to fix their shots, pour their drams, agitate their preferred reserve, top up their sweating Glencairn glasses, he encountered some difficulties dissociating the locus of their authority with their poison of choice. When he suggested that the wheezy bench liars might try diversifying their palates once in a while, they eyeballed him like he'd just silently loosened a testicle into eyeshot. He knew not to nettle or filibuster them with campaigns of liquid betterment for too long, lest they call on the Tyrant's proprietor to sort out Briggs's mouth or dock his wages; he wasn't one of the girls with their foaming black tresses and cheap perfume, for he was no more valuable to them than the human furniture expected to shut up when a king pauses at the threshold to his throne room.

When they were in the throes of drinking their whiskey, the old geezers would suddenly disengage from their heated discussion, as if in hushed reverence. Or if not reverence, then admiration, the way a breeder inspects a pedigree thoroughbred. Briggs had never known any table-downed liquor to have that effect, not least the same drink for an entire sortie of dissimilar shrink-wrapped souls, but whiskey proved the great democratiser, because even a king might sit mystified by the play of light on breastplate gold. The geezers were in veneration of not merely how their beloved tincture tasted, but of the way it sharpened their minds at the moment of swallowing, the way it made a fist of their gut at a moment's flowering, weaponising the fire in their veins until their bodies were dancing quick enough to evade the blow of betrayal.

For the old bloodhounds forgathered in the backrooms of The Brass Tyrant, whiskey in the throat was like divulging the scent of a fox. Blood glowed in their snouts. Hackles bristled in rebellion. Nostrils dilated to divine the tang of enemy sweat, the smut of a too-sudden exit. The drink restored their senses, before it clouded them and its temporary advantages had to be renewed. It was clear the geezers imbibed their premium 100-proof corn spirit session whiskeys because they'd persuaded themselves it enhanced their Bugsy Siegel-like insight, their inner Iago, a fortification which inured them to the quiet psychosis that every swinging dick within an immediate ten-mile radius was angling to fuck them. There were things foxes could hear which the old bloodhounds were ill-equipped to intercept or transceive, whispers which the gnarls of the corner stoop, the fissures in the manhole covers, the gutters like envelopes of light, the bleached marquee of the neighbourhood fruit shop refused to disclose. It took a convoluted web of spies, a skyline of hired eyes, what a single stave of syrup whiskey could divulge with the right acuity of mind. The geezers were willing to wait it out.

They'd nurse their steins and snifters, croaking in symphony like a grove of crows, and wait for the seed of inspiration to worm its way into their beady black skulls, a syzygy of their knotted minds, a clairvoyance activated from incidental articles. Then it'd announce itself in the way one geezer might trill to another: *Did you see the way Little Giotto, Vito's kid, flinched when Don Fabrizio inquired about his missing brother last week?* And his balding *consigliére* would listen with a sage curl of the lips, while drawing a quart of Blanton's between his teeth, before clucking: *Who? You mean Nicky Santorini? That* schecchino's *had it coming. And I'd trust that* scocciamento *punk, Giotto, about as far as a nickel'll take a gondola in Naples.*

The geezers tended to repel covert intrusion. At first, after a few weeks of concerted analysis from beneath the rack of wineglasses, it occurred to Briggs that the girls had been deigned the sole exception; they could move wherever their curiosity determined, and it rankled the geezers not at all: for a satellite to conduct a comprehensive reconnaissance it must be allowed a freewheeling orbit. And yet from the day Briggs had finagled his first shift at The Tyrant, he'd found his roving eye consistently entranced by the gold-lustred spinet piano stationed at the rear of the bar, a marled Wurlitzer organ which had sauntered out of esteem sometime in the 40's, but which throbbed from within a matt-coat of red lacquer as though the Devil's own pocket-sized armoury. It reminded him of something you'd find whittled in miniature, buried in the sand of a lion-fish tank.

When he'd initially spotted the spinet piano, Briggs had decided that it must've been installed out of a last-minute scuffle for ornamentation, because there was nothing else like it in the bar, and there was no evidence to suggest the owners of The Tyrant were the inheritors of a musical legacy. But once a day, sometime after 12, the rear door to the establishment would chunk against the grille of frost outside and admit entrance to a short man with august features attired in a linen suit of coolest lilac. His eyes were flinty, his cheekbones were strikingly faceted, his whiskers were bouquets of white-and-black barbs, and his brow stormily clove by the brim of a teal bowler cut from Japanese felt which he would collapse against his knee the minute the Gravesend winter manifested him at the threshold. Threaded in his lapel, the man in the linen suit would promenade a different blossom for every day of the week. When Briggs set to mentally cataloguing these, however, he quickly surmised that the man gravitated towards fragrant perennials, fluted specimens like violets, irises, cyclamen, long-stemmed roses. Once, he'd adorned his buttonhole with a French marigold, which made him look as though he'd been shot in the chest, its tufted petals like the fuselage exposed when a bull gores a *gaucho.* These seemed only to correspond to the mood of the man in the linen suit; if there was a criminal semaphore being implemented here, Briggs could not decipher it, leastways not without a floral calendar to study; but it did not matter, for the man in the linen suit would telegraph how he was feeling on any given day to the assembled clientele of The

Tyrant by his ministrations at the piano.

The man would call on Briggs or, if he was not available, any of the bartenders able to disentangle themselves from flirtations with The Tyrant's female patrons the quickest, and he would order an iced finger of whiskey with a slap of coins on the bar, before pivoting toward the pianoforte with drink in hand, to assume his command post from behind its sleek cherrywood contours. He'd relinquish both his hat and his drink to its firelit simmer on the gabled edge of the piano top over a silver handkerchief of silk. He would remove the gold band from his wedding finger and ensconce it in his waistcoat pocket, permit his hands to linger over the keys of the dormant instrument, and sleepily close his wry grey eyes.

On certain weeks, Briggs might have to work both the morning and the evening of the same day, and instead of returning home in the interim he would occasionally resolve to occupy himself by frequenting the local Korean repertory theatre, secreted on 6th Avenue in Sunset Park, before his split-shift kicked in; it was there in the rumple of warmth afforded him by the suppurated cinema upholstery, while without the city was jack-o'-lanterned by snarls of ice, that he first discovered the films of the storied Japanese masters, of Mizoguchi, of Kurosawa, of Yasujirō Ozu, in sensuous 35mm monochrome restorations: and it was to the venerable and mercurial souls populating these silver satiny-grained dreamscapes, to Chishû Ryû in *Late Spring* or Takashi Shimura in *Ikiru* or Masayuki Mori in *Ugetsu*, that Briggs quietly likened The Tyrant's own man in lilac. To Briggs, the pianist at the spinet possessed something of the same equestrian gravity, the same porcelain features and condemnatory gaze, the same untroubled brow and yet the same dark torqued jaw that he associated with the sumptuous screen dramas of Nihon's Golden Age. When the man in lilac had succumbed to his startled fugue state before the piano's teeth, he would slump forward with a nearly indiscernible servitude and slowly, as if in the throes of mystification, his face would soften. Only then would he play his music. Somehow, in the magicked impetus of such a moment, Briggs could swear that the glyph of whiskey left untasted on the piano's vertex seemed to glow still more brightly as the man in lilac commenced to perform; and Briggs understood this to be both asinine and nightmarish, yet still the impression prevailed, that the man summoned up a colour in the liquor he'd installed on the spinet top which had not been heretofore observed. As he played, the tiny gargle of toasty bourbon went about its alchemical moult, became endowed with the gold optics of a saber drawn at sundown, less drink than trinket, the heart carved out of an angel. The man in lilac played on, the sockets of his cheeks seized in a frowning rictus, and the old bloodhounds at the bar would retire their drunken calumnies and listen in with appreciative faces, sweeten their mouths with a drop of favourite oak, and disarm their ears of their spikier secrets, submitting their minds to nocturnes which seethed in minor-chord like bells used to navigate gator-clouded waters.

There swelled such a maelstrom of sound from within the fretwork mechanism of the whirring pianoforte, such a sound of pine-cradled gladness, of woodpeckers in frissons of quarrelsome lust, of squires in chainmail twinkling in tandem beneath the domed ceiling of mist-swathed redwoods, of swains and archers brisking the heavy foliage as they disbursed, of dragons and armadillos making home in temperate auracarian roosts. The tinkle of the pianist's fingers summoned up quivers in the skulls of the old priestly listeners. The music flushed Briggs of his expertly-rehearsed stoicism; love for an unadulterated simplicity, for a sound of light seething, for the first instance of a poet being weaned on the coil of the rain, seized his insides until he felt free and obedient, miraculously free. The pianist incited a fever in Briggs, a glow he'd resigned himself to no longer linger in, now that he was brave enough to settle for a life of small significance.

He'd been okay with it, too, until now; had been teaching himself how to succumb to smalltime suckitude, to a plight of sedate dereliction. After the pain of his family falling apart, of losing his sister, of vacating his home city, Briggs had fancied a spell of inconsequential amusement would be enough. He'd permitted himself to first defy, and then recoil at the thunder of ambition, its ominous light show in the eyes of strivers and coat-tailers. He'd resolved himself to invite contentment from behind the teak of a Gravesend bar, had reckoned with it annulling any unshaken and unplumbed designs he might have retained for himself from before his sister was taken by the state, and his life changed. Briggs had even discovered in New York a semblance of prevailing anonymity. He could've rewritten himself as a wallflower, as a cipher seeking quiet surrender. He would've only needed a few more months of counting change, waxing floorboards, pulling beers, reconciling the register, loping home after midnight in the snow. But the music summoned by the man in the linen suit compelled Briggs into fits of reeling temper; he found himself harried by renewed aspirations as he listened to the sveltely-attired minstrel at the spinet piano, possessed by remote notions of eminence, of danger, of arrogance founded, of masculine grandeur elegantly tailored in lilac.

The man's music shucked him clean as he listened with a squint beside the rheumy old geezers, flensed him of a jellied grey substance that was probably his peace-of-mind. Briggs felt newly cloven; there was plenty of room beneath his ribcage for more of the pianist's ivory, heat and steel. Of course, he recognised the man in the linen suit as a gangster like the others—the one thing the Jersey streets hadn't fostered in Briggs was selective blindness—but no incognito crook subsisting on embezzled annuities and New York mozzarella slice should be capable of apprehending such airy and evanescent melodies, no heavy hands so precise in weaving rhapsodies and overtures and sonatas in miniature. This was the genius of the man in the linen suit: he appeared to straddle worlds in stark contrast with each other, and expertly too: as a hand-to-mouth malefactor he was refined; as a patrician member of the New York *cognoscenti*, he was a little unscrupulous, a little cloak-and-dagger in his demeanour and his business for any other socialites to compete. The man arrayed himself with a gothic longevity at the coralline red piano, a Hammer Horror rapacity which conveyed likenesses of vampire maestros in Briggs's mind, the swimmily-coiffured kin of Karloff, of Lugosi, of Vincent Price enveloped in the wings of an instrument which seemed to dribble and buck beneath his diffident petting. Briggs got accustomed to folding his arms at the bar, with his eyes narrowed, a surliness about the mouth while he remained witness to The Brass Tyrant's transformation.

Soon, no sooner than it took for the pianist's hushful glosses along the spinet's keys to swell into their chiming refrain, no sooner had the bar's cowed clientele withdrawn to memories of yesteryear's threnody, a music to remind the half-deaf of half-ripe music which sweetened the air when they were younger and given to quick brooding lusts, no sooner had new chords become subsumed by a bath of calm white fire, that the venue was enveilled in a golden arch of surf-hewn sound, a glowing bower of wind-combed clangour which carved a roof overhead, beneath which Briggs felt his body lighten and begin to hover of its own free logic. Briggs saw how the man in the linen suit imprisoned his listeners with golden lassitudes of colliding octaves; he drew up the plans for each jail of the mind, and praised you with pretty fugues as you built up the walls to contain yourself. He kept you castellated in reverie, fucked-up with mute stupefaction. Everyone allowed themselves to be beset by a guileful beauty. Then the man in the raiment of purple linen and grey nankeen would fell his own bower, would stand and desist and reclaim his fingers with a surgical clap of the lid. The piano would discover itself muffled, like a bear kept captive to perform its grotesque dance and then return to its tortured confinement. Bang would fall the whiskey dram, warped would work its passage down the pianist's neck. Slap would go his knuckles as they scorned the piano's armoured hide! Up would work the rosy moods from their alveoli sacs beneath the skin. Red would blaze the brilliant heat of the drink scaling his aged face. Wide would oscillate his bright evil eyes. Sure would curl his odious grin, and to Briggs he would point, and to Briggs he would beckon.

'Well colour me astonished if this sumphole of sin hasn't yet collapsed with you foul colony of rat bastards gnawing out its foundations from under it! I should say I'm glad I braved the snow to check in on this warren of pestilence, because it'd be a little indelicate for the NYPD to have to come bag and tag body parts when they'd find chewed-up articles of your neighbour mixed amidst walls of shit. Let's suppress those cannibal instincts, you gummy old vermin fucks, and apply ourselves to administering the cure! Barkeep! A whiskey apiece for the toothy sewer-jockeys and wriggling waste-tasters at the bar! And don't schtupp me on the quality there, muscles, because I mean to gargle down your house barrel blend too, and I don't wanna be hoiking up rodent droppings like pomegranate stones!'

The Brass Tyrant would entertain this same bellowy exegesis, or a variation of it, every second or third day. It never failed to bore and antagonise Briggs in equal measure, nor erode his ever-resonating interest in gaining the man in linen's approval, nor diminish his ambition to ensnare the man in a quiet inglenook and demand somehow to be cut in on the action. Briggs would nod and keep eye contact, would decant the perfect shot, would exhale like an obedient horse, would jot down the tab with a scholarly flourish, would continue waiting in eyeshot, would contrive it so that he always appeared busy enough not to be reprimanded but disposed enough to appear dormant, in need of a secret directive. One day Briggs decided to risk it; he figured he'd never curry favour with the bloodhounds if he didn't at least demonstrate the appetite to be recognised, to be granted an audience at the heart of the pack. An hour before the man in the linen suit was due to materialise for his daily interlude at the spinet, Briggs scrawled a handwritten note and sandwiched it between the hairline crack of the piano lid and the organ's glinting teeth.

Though the culmination of several weeks' vacillation, the decision that day had been a spontaneous one, and had thus stymied Briggs for any Damascene in-the-moment inspiration; he found he didn't have much to say when it got right down to it, so he deliberately sought not to court embellishment. His envoy to the man in the linen suit was therefore shocking in its economy. It read: *My name is Briggs—I tend bar. You call me "muscles". You seem to know your way about. I intend to work for you. You hiring?*

That afternoon, the gangster in lilac arrived on the limens to the Tyrant in a smoking jacket, conjured with a boutonnière of a single red carnation in his breast, his arm snaked around the willowy waist of a woman so extraordinarily beautiful Briggs felt something chunk inside him like a token palmed into a nickelodeon's coin slot. A whirring seized his innards, a scratchy song installed in shellac and vinyl commenced its tinny orchestration in the spaces between his ears. He wasn't one for identifying or acknowledging beauty; he'd been born a romantic in the airiest sense of the word, but not, it had appeared, for admiring feminine grace. Oftentimes, Briggs was more attracted to ugly girls, or at least girls whom the world or the women themselves had conspired to uglify in some way: he didn't believe much in poetry, and preferred studying the other sex for their earthy realism, for the lengths to which a grown-ass female would revolt against the fawning of the patriarchy. He was consequently aroused by women who neither appreciated his affection nor warranted it: they were frequently either academic in their application to love, and therefore disinterested in Briggs's overwrought gestures of tenderness; or else they were boastful fucks, anti-monogamists who invited a rutting with pacts of exclusivity that were rarely redeemable outside the day they were forged. So the Farrah-headed vision on the lilac gangster's arm was something to behold for Briggs—beauty that refused to be equivocated in poetry.

She emerged into the light backlit by the tempest white of Brooklyn's snowy skull, vespers rising off her body as though her trespass had sprung from the eye socket of the city. She moved like the Devil's answer to a barn owl, eyes like sulphur-blown glass facets in her head, cheekbones like marble wings, rasps of dragon breath swathing her honey complexion as though arrayed in autumnal plumage. Briggs watched on as she shook herself free of a leather lambskin stole, her head crowned in a cloche hat knit from a silver fox pelt, her hair slinking round her throat like the twined talons of a raptor of the desert sands.

She was Italian, he saw, blonde like the Milanese tryst-cravers who congregated in plazas, laundromats, lighthouse doorways on the covers of every erotic pulp novel Briggs had ever spotted in a subway spinny rack. She glided as she moved, and Briggs finally noticed that on her wrist there teemed a corsage of spider chrysanthemum florets and maidenhair fern sprigs; when contrast with the gangster's carnation the effect was almost venomous, scarlet and green. They each gravitated towards the bar, the pianist and his sleepy-mouthed moll in her fleeced-fox hat, and Briggs knew then the threat of control invoked in owning to your convictions when he croaked an arid greeting to the couple and asked what they were having, and The Manticore's face seemed to transform in an instant, and from within his tigerish grin there boomed a voice like that of a gondolier, and the voice spoke a single word, and that word was “Whiskey”.

WORLD PEACE 3

by Gustavo Alberto Garcia Vaca

---

declaration of more
thank battalion
empathy squadron
renaissance mission
arty brigade
farmed resistance
mind field
dropping calms
pensive offensive
weapons of mass construction

VISITATION

by Gustavo Alberto Garcia Vaca

Love is falling in drops of rain that scatter along the streets.
Tender embraces are falling on the roofs of houses.
The tunnels of the subway are being flooded by strange affections.
Birds of a thousand colors dance through the heavens.
The day and the night arrive with smooth songs.
Butterflies signal the order of our offerings.
Joy cascades in blue rivers.
The air is cleansed by the breezes that arrive to teach us.

LADY KILLER

by Monika McGreal Viola

The killing ritual was always the same—spot one and, overcome by hatred and disgust, dash to the bookcase for a tome thick enough, squint her eyes and slam the book against the wall. In this way, she killed it swiftly, more humanely, for both involved.

The removal of the splattered remains was what terrified her. After the book fell, and the creature's legs and body were pressed flat against the wall, she couldn't bring herself to remove the specimen: what if she scooped it up in a tissue and felt the outline of its fractured body? True, it was less than ideal to have her apartment encrusted with dead arachnids and leggy insects—but they were dead, mummified, relics. Relish seeing them, she did not, but she was satisfied in the knowledge that they could no longer quick-step into her path. The deceased creepy-crawlers were gruesome, but controlled.

She lived in a big city, as luck would have it, and insect-infested apartments were an everyday part of life. Rightly so, her collection—her *décor*—inhibited her social life; she certainly didn't have the freedom to invite friends or dates to her home. And also, there was the problem of the fallen books, a quandary to which she gave considerable thought. Although her apartment was lined with books—specifically those once belonging to her mother—these held much in the way of sentimental value and were not to be used in the sport of bug squelching. She began to purchase throwaway softcovers: cheap thrillers, Harlequin romances, hackneyed best sellers with wonderfully thick spines and filled with pages of useless chatter. These she stacked on their own separate shelf and, when one had served its lethal purpose, swept out the fire escape it went. She always checked first, of course, to ensure no unsuspecting pedestrian strolled below.

One day, while shopping for vegetables, she met a man. They had chanced upon the bin of cauliflower at the same moment, and he offered to hold her plastic bag open while she selected the vegetables of her choice. She was not one to be particular about her cauliflower, but the man appeared so magnanimous as he set down his own shopping basket to assist her, that she took her time with the little white clusters, hemming and hawing as he patiently offered his advice. As they waited on the checkout line, he asked if he might take her to a baseball game, and she accepted.

He took her to the baseball game. And then to dinner, to the farmer's market on Sunday, and to the opening of the Museum of Furniture Design. She didn't particularly like the Museum of Furniture Design; she felt it lacked variety. All the chairs seemed to have one leg, and all the tables seemed to be made of colored plastic. She preferred more traditional styles, like white wooden rocking chairs with woven-straw seats. But he explained to her the importance of the modern furniture movement, and she understood after that.

One night, after the movies, the man walked her home while he discussed the gruesome feature they had watched. She didn't mind violence as a rule, but this particular film contained such a great deal of butchering, slaughtering, and scalping that she had constantly needed to avert her eyes. The hero—who, coincidentally, was also the killer—seemed to derive extreme satisfaction from his work of slicing and dicing people to bits. He smiled serenely, blissfully, as the blood splattered his face. She had been surprised to see the man gazing ardently at the screen, his eyes bulging wide and his lip twitching as he shoveled popcorn into his mouth. He explained to her how intriguing the camera work was and how it manipulated the viewer's eye and urged her to focus on the camera angles as well. That made the film unique, he continued as they left the theater. That made sense, and she marveled at how the director had managed to capture a bug's eye view of the world.

At her building, they lingered. He asked if she would invite him in for a cup of coffee. Fearful of what he might think of her and how she lived, she feigned exhaustion. He reminded her that caffeine was the very remedy for tiredness. She argued that

she would prefer to tidy up first. He insisted that he didn't mind. He would not be swayed, and she found herself without an excuse. Now knowing this to be their last date, she looked at him fondly and said she would invite him in for a cup of tea instead, for that was all she had.

Up the flight of stairs to her apartment. On the landing, she lingered. She traced her finger along the banister, dillydallying. She jiggled her key, opened her door, and turned on the light. He said nothing, instead walked straight in and nodded as he looked around, then settled himself on the couch.

Do you have Earl Grey, he asked her. She shook her head no. Only chamomile.

Get some Earl Grey, he said, blind to the dismembered bodies smeared on the walls around him.

After that night, the man began to visit every day. He often brought with him gifts, small tokens of his affection for her. He got her a fancy electric mixer because he said he knew how much she must love to cook. He got her a very expensive pair of Italian knives, which she considered particularly thoughtful; he had himself recommended new ones—it seemed her old ones were inadequate for cutting vegetables—and now, she didn't have to go to the trouble of choosing them herself. What was wonderful about these gifts was how the man never seemed to need a particular reason to give them. He would arrive at her door with a box in tow, and how romantic it felt to receive gifts on a 'just because' basis.

After several months, however, she did begin to worry—as women will do, he chided—that the man was losing interest in her. Although he came to her apartment daily, she had yet to see where he lived. He told her he lived with roommates. She told him it would be nice to meet his roommates, or any of his friends and family. He assured her that she would be fully incorporated into his life.

We can discuss this again in another six months, he said. She marked this on the white desk calendar he had given her, excited to have set a date.

Then there was that one day he said to her,

You've got a spider crawling on the wall, mind if I kill it?

No, she said. With the beginnings of a smile on his face, he crept up to the arachnid and banged it with a signed copy of *The Blind Assassin*. He smashed it again, and again, squishing and twisting the bug into place. Satisfied, he removed a tissue from his coat, wiped the wall clean, examined the tissue, then put it back into his pocket. She stared at the wall. A slight stain was visible; however, it was a marked improvement over the rest of her apartment.

Missed a spot, he said, going to the kitchen. He returned with a roll of paper towels. With a fresh towel, he wiped another bug from the wall, this time one she had killed herself.

Darn thing won't come off, he said and cleaned yet another section of the wall. This continued until the entire wall was devoid of the bugs she had slain over the years.

The next morning, the man brought over two cups of coffee and a can of paint, and coated the walls a sparkling white.

I left a stain yesterday, he said. She told him she understood. The day after that, he arrived with an exterminator's gun.

What would you do if I weren't here? He sprayed until no insect would dare scamper within a hundred meters of the apartment.

What a change! And what an odd sensation to find oneself freed. She often would sit on her couch and stare at the stark white walls. She thought about hanging some art—she had wanted to buy gold-gilded frames and hang reproductions of Giotto's masterpieces. She loved the classic Italian paintings and had often envisioned traipsing around Florence, staying in *pensiones* that overlooked the Arno, secretly fancying herself a Miss Honeychurch. How disappointed she was to discover this view to be incorrect. Pre-Renaissance art was passé, he explained to her. The minimalist movement was *en vogue* at the present. Artwork on the walls would clutter her apartment. She was grateful to have someone like this man in her life, someone willing to tell her when she committed a faux pas.

Then there was also the day when she came home to find her mother's books stacked in boxes—he had packed them all away. What's this, she asked.

He stood in front of her shelves, placing down navy blue books with a methodical thud. He hummed all the while, and the combination of the two sounds was not unlike the whirring of cicadas on a late spring afternoon.

You're home early, he scolded. I have a gift for you.

She stared at her bookcases, stacked in alphabetical order.

But those are encyclopedias, she said.

Collector's edition. He tweaked her nose as he passed by.

My mother's books, she said. My mother's books, she said again.

You silly goose, he sighed. After all the trouble I've taken to fix everything, he told her.

It would hurt his feelings not to accept such a gift. She supposed her bookcases had been a mess. She supposed she was lucky to have someone who noticed such things.

Still… sometimes… she was overcome by the prickly loneliness of her blindingly unadorned apartment. At night, when the distractions of the day slid away, she had taken to angling her desk lamp toward the wall like a spotlight. Then, she would wiggle her fingers in the path of the light, creating shadows along the walls. She took comfort in these shadowed shapes and soon, every night she fell asleep commanding the black silhouettes as they scampered across her room.

As time traipsed on, the man did more and more for her. No more tedious trips to the outdoor market on Saturdays or the farmers market on Sundays. She had discovered that, despite her earlier ambivalence, cooking seemed to be a passion of hers and thus devoted her time to perfecting the craft. He bought her several cookbooks, and she studied these in the mornings, then attempted to prepare something delicious in the evenings. She wasn't successful, but he assured her that, with practice, she couldn't help but improve.

One afternoon, while laying out the ingredients for a sponge cake, she saw a spider crawling on the outside screen of the kitchen window. When was the last time she had met anything like it? From inside her white-walled apartment, she felt an unfamiliar longing. She didn't like this creature; she knew this to be true by her shuddered cringe. But the fear came from within her, belonged to her. Unclasping the screen at the bottom of the window, she pushed it open half an inch or so. She trembled as the spider slowly made its way through the opening… then returned to her ingredients.

Later that night, the man worked in the living room, installing his latest gift. As he meticulously fastened a one-legged chair to the floor, she heard him curse. She wiped her floury hands on the paisley apron he had bought her earlier in the week.

Stand back, he said. There's a spider in the house, and I don't want you upsetting yourself.

He bent down with his face close to the floor, attempting to keep his prey in sight as it crawled in and out of the light flung on the wall by the table lamp. His back was arched high, and his knees stuck out as he crouched. His legs jerked ever so slightly—she never before had noticed how spindly he was. His hair spiked out in all different directions, casting varying peaks of shadow on the walls. His knobby elbows jutted back, ready to spring down in attack. It was his face, however, that fascinated her. Lips curled and twitching and eyebrows arched down, he frowned so fiercely she could barely recognize his features. He looked misshapen, deformed, hideous even, and not unlike…

Overwhelmed with hatred and disgust, she dashed to the bookcase for a tome thick enough. She picked up an encyclopedia, volume ABC. Squinting her eyes, she slammed the book hard against the wall, squishing the man flat. She opened her eyes. She banged again with the book. She did this again, and again, squishing and twisting him into place until he was pressed flat upon the wall. Finally, she stopped, letting the book fall to the floor as she took a deep breath.

She knew the stain would ruin her new white walls. But, truth be told, she had missed the old spots.

WHAT THE LIVING DO

(*Novel Excerpt*)

by Susan E. Wadds

A turkey vulture drops a rope of intestine and lifts away into a hard blue sky. The dog at the roadside is some kind of mixed breed with a delicate snout and brindled coat. Mel eases the truck to a stop, and I clamp on my hardhat.

Overhead, the big bird carves a dark circle while Mel drags the shovel out of the truck bed. Even though I know the dog is dead, I squat to touch it just in case, but its jaw gapes, its legs are stiff as branches, and its milky eyes are open.

Michelangelo peeled the skins of cadavers. He was searching for a deeper mystery than how muscle attaches to bone. I am searching for something more too; not just a tag to name the owner of a dog. In the dead, Michelangelo found the underpinnings for his art. I haven't yet been able to name what it is I find in these still creatures.

There's no tag on this dog. He's scrawny. I touch a rib bone that pokes through the skin like a tire spoke. Was he abandoned or did he simply leave, the scent of wild things pulling him from the safety of home?

Mel drives a boot on to the shovel's edge and begins to dig. The crunch of hard-packed summer dirt, the scent of forgotten things deep in the earth, the steady rasping pulse of Mel's breathing.

We didn't bury my sister, Goldie, or my father. After the fire they brought two clay urns to the edge of the Kootenay River. The wind picked up the ash and bits of bone, casting them in a wide arc over the cold river. Before they settled into the water, a gust of wind caught a handful of ash and flung it into my mouth.

When we slide the dog into the hole, its skull bone shows white through the cracked bowl of his head. This doesn't cause me to gag the way it used to. I still smell smoke, though, whenever the dull moon of an eye lies exposed like this.

Mel labors onto one knee and opens his fist, letting a confetti of tobacco drift over the small corpse. I keep my eyes on the still form while Mel lifts his head to intone a prayer. I hear *"nimoosh"* and *"miigwech,"* the words for "dog" and "thank you."

The first roadkill I buried was a fox. Nothing about it seemed dead that cool spring morning. It was as if the fox had simply lain down to rest in the middle of the Second Line, the white tip of its tail curled over the sun flare of its body. I'd sensed Mel's eyes on me even though he faced straight ahead. I'd removed my gloves to search for a pulse and found a hardness that made me rock back on my heels.

"Waagosh," Mel had said.

The fox smelled of juniper and cedar. Turning my head away so Mel couldn't see my face, I'd heard the shovel's metal-on-metal across the truck sides.

It was the prayer that undid me, the soft syllables like a lullaby.

Once we were back in the truck, Mel touched a finger to the box of tissues tucked into the console and started the engine. When he'd turned to the left to check for traffic, I yanked one from the box and made as if checking traffic from the right.

Mel is the only one I ever want to ride with; the only one who's never made lame lunges to grab my ass on the pretense of helping me into the cab, and the only one who doesn't bitch - not about the weather, the road conditions, or his wife, and not even about the cutbacks that have forced us to drive the snowplows without a wingman.

After we've mounded the earth and tamped it down over the young dog, I toss the shovel into the truck bed and step up into the cab. Mel has the truck in gear.

"Teach me how to pray, Mel," I say.

Without turning his head, Mel lifts a gray eyebrow.

"You pray to real things, like animals. I need you to teach me."

His answer comes like it always does, after a long pause. "Don't pray *to* animals. Pray *for* them." Now he turns a half turn, almost facing me. "To give thanks."

I want some of what he has; that steady sweeping gaze over the land, the ease with which he dangles his fingers through the steering wheel, the slow nod when one of the good old boys at the yard calls him Chief. "Is that what makes you peaceful?"

"Peaceful?" he says as if trying out the word.

"Yeah," I say. "How does it start? It sounds like bonjour."

"*Boozhoo*," he corrects. "We say, *Boozhoo Gzheminido.* Means, Hello Creator."

"The other things you say – after that?"

Mel nods, returns his gaze to the road. "*Mshkiki nini ndizhinikaaz,* is how I start."

I try out the words but they feel like pebbles in my mouth. And it looks like Mel is trying not to smile.

"What?"

"You said, 'My name is Strong Earth Man.'"

"Well, I like that. How do you say, 'My name is Strong Earth Woman'?"

The smile that was forming vanishes.

There are these times when I feel I've stepped over some sacred invisible boundary. It's in the density of his quiet, as if all the light has been sucked into a vacuum. "What did I say?"

I lean the side of my head into the window and see through the outside mirror that we've done a fine job. Not even a ripple in the gravel remains to mark the spot where the dog is buried. In the beginning, I'd try to insist we find the owners, but if the animals weren't close to a house, the mandate was simply to bury them. No time to go calling door to door.

"Mel, what should I say?"

Easing his foot from the pedal, Mel turns the truck back onto the road. "Just your name."

"Can't I have a cool name too?"

We're on the road heading south, on the lookout for roadkill, bent signs, and potholes. Sun comes hot and thick through the heavy leaves of maple, oak, and poplar. When Mel doesn't answer, I turn to look full at him. His eyes are closed for a bit too long.

"Mel? How do I get a name like that?"

His eyelids lift and it seems to take some effort for him to focus. He blinks. The fingers dangling from the top of the steering wheel tap at air.

I've screwed things up; the long silence makes that clear. I want to apologize but I'm not exactly sure for what. "Okay, so no special name, okay. So how do I say it with the name I've got?"

The hard line of Mel's jaw softens. "You say your name, then *ndizhinikaaz*."

The sharp sound of my own name is jarring when followed by the warmth of the Ojibwe syllables. I want a name that's tough and wild, like Cougar Woman. But given that the man I live with is that much younger than I am, it might not be the best choice. And given that my request has been met with Mel's inscrutable silence, I decide not to push it. After a second attempt at 'Brett *ndizhinikaaz*' I say, "What do you say next?"

From under his eyelids, Mel watches ahead through the sun-stained windshield. "I say, Rama *ndoonjibaa, waawaashkeshi doodem.*"

This invocation flows like a song, warms me right into my belly, where it's been cold for some time. "Does that mean, 'I'm from Rama'?"

Mel nods.

"And the rest?"

"My clan."

"You have a clan? What kind of clan?"

"Deer."

On the far side of the road, guard posts list toward the ditch, their guide wires stretched tight.

"There it is," I say, pointing.

"I don't have a clan," I say as Mel swings the truck around in a smooth U. "So what would come next for me?"

"Just where you're from, then *ndoonjibaa.*"

"Where I'm from?"

"Where your heart is," Mel says.

"But they're not the same place," I say.

For the rest of the afternoon Mel and I are mostly silent. That's what I like about him. Once when I asked him why he never asked questions, he told me if a person wanted to tell a thing, they would. When I said that inquiring after the well-being of people you care about was supposed to be the polite thing to do, he just shook his head.

I push on my sunglasses to combat the glare that blazes through the pocked windshield and content myself with watching for potholes to fill and signs to straighten.

"I read somewhere that it's going to be a mild winter," I say.

Mel glances out his window.

When he doesn't comment, I say, "Late start. That would be good."

We have the windows open. Neither of us likes air-conditioning, even when it's this hot. A few strands of hair have broken loose from my braid and whip across my mouth. I don't want to think about winter, but when I close my eyes I see snow, ice, sand and brine. A dark empty road and an almost empty hopper. Alone at three in the morning stuffed into my padded coveralls, the drone of engine, the steady scrape of blade, lights – in my rear view, overhead, ahead, blue, red, white – and coming down that hill on glare ice. At the low dip a little blue car revolved like something at a fall fair. I flip open my eyes and resolve anew my pledge to get out before winter sets in.

I'm used to waiting for Mel to answer. When we first started riding together, I'd fill in the quiet by answering for him or asking more questions. Because it finally registered that when I did that he never actually answered, I've trained myself to wait. Now I like the waiting. It's as if the world stops just then and my mind goes still, too.

A slow smile forms on his face. "Once, Web, my older brother, told me we were in for a cold winter. He said you could tell because the caterpillars had thick coats." Mel scratches the sparse stubble on his chin. His smile fades. "I laughed. I thought he was joking."

"He wasn't? That's how you can tell?"

Only Mel's eyes move to take a quick look at me. "Maybe," he says, flicking on the turn signal and spinning the wheel to the right.

"How do the caterpillars look this year?"

His smile is a smaller version of the one a moment before. "It's still hot. Maybe check in September."

Mel and I replace three road signs perforated with bullet holes, coldpatch half a dozen potholes, remove a fallen ash off a county road and pull a mattress from a ditch. No more dead things today.

At the yard, Mel tips the brim of the ball cap that has replaced his hardhat and we get into our respective vehicles – me in my Yaris, he in "Pony", his Dodge van that he's snazzed up for camping at pow wows.

CONTRIBUTORS

BARBARA DADDINO

Barbara Daddino holds an MFA from NYU where she studied under E.L. Doctorow, Breyten Breytenbach, and Francine Prose. She has taught English and creative writing in the Suffolk County school system and creative writing at NYU as an adjunct. Her essays and movie reviews have appeared in *Newsday* and on PBS. She was also featured in two PBS interviews about late-life divorce. She is currently working on a novel inspired by her story, "Floaters," a finalist in *Glimmer Train's* New Writers' Short Story Contest. She lives in Shoreham, Long Island where she works in a tower overlooking the Sound. From there, it is easy to hear the hag singing.

WILLIAM DORESKI

William Doreski lives in Peterborough, New Hampshire, in a small house in the woods. He taught at Keene State College for many years, but has now retired to feed the deer and wild turkeys. He has published three critical studies, including *Robert Lowell's Shifting Colors*. His essays, poetry, fiction, and reviews have appeared in many journals and several small-press books. His forthcoming book of poetry is *The Last Concert* (Salmon Press).

LAURA CESARCO EGLIN

Laura Cesarco Eglin is the author of three collections of poetry, *Llamar al agua por su nombre* (Mouthfeel Press, 2010), *Sastrería* (Yaugurú, 2011), and *Los brazos del saguaro* (Yaugurú, 2015). A bilingual edition of her first book translated by Scott Spanbauer was published as *Calling Water by Its Name* (Mouthfeel Press, 2016). A selection of poems from Sastería was translated collaboratively into English with Teresa Williams, and subsequently published as the chapbook *Tailor Shop: Threads* (Finishing Line Press, 2013). Cesarco Eglin also published the chapbook *Occasions to Call Miracles Appropriate* (Lunamopolis, The Lune series, 2015). Her poems and translations have appeared or are forthcoming in a variety of journals, including *Modern Poetry in Translation, MiPOesias, Eleven Eleven, Puerto del Sol, Copper Nickel, Arsenic Lobster, International Poetry Review, Tupelo Quarterly, Columbia Poetry Review, Timber, Pretty Owl Poetry, Pilgrimage, Periódico de Poesía, Metrópolis,* and more. Her poems are also featured in the Uruguayan women's section of *Palabras Errantes, Plusamérica: Latin American Literature in Translation*. Cesarco Eglin's poetry appears in *América invertida: An Anthology of Emerging Uruguayan Poets* (University of New Mexico Press, 2016). She is the co-founding editor and publisher of Veliz Books.

NANCY FLYNN

Nancy Flynn grew up on the Susquehanna River in northeastern Pennsylvania, spent many years on a downtown creek in Ithaca, New York, and now lives near the mighty Columbia in Portland, Oregon. She attended Oberlin College, Cornell University, and has an M.A. in English from SUNY/Binghamton. Her writing has received an Oregon Literary Fellowship and the James Jones First Novel Fellowship. Poetry chapbooks include *The Hours of Us* (2007) and *Eternity a Coal's Throw* (2012);

her book-length collection, *Every Door Recklessly Ajar*, was published by Cayuga Lake Books in June 2015. Her website is www.nancyflynn.com.

DANNY JUDGE

Danny Judge's short fiction has appeared in many literary journals, most recently *Twisted Vine, Flash Fiction Magazine, Burningword*, and *Lunch Ticket*, for which he is nominated for a 2016 Pushcart Prize. He is a freelance copywriter and the founding Editor of *The Indianola Review*, a quarterly print journal.

MARK P. LAWLEY

Mark P. Lawley is the grown-up guy version of Moana. He writes fiction, composes music, and codes software. His work has been recognized by *Ploughshares, Zoetrope: All-Story, Glimmer Train, Nimrod, The Southwest Review*, and *Shenandoah*. He lives in Charleston, South Carolina with his wife and two bunny rabbits. You can read more at marklawley.com or tweet him a line @MarkPLawley.

JOSEPH LISOWSKI

Joseph Lisowski was Professor of English at the University of the Virgin Islands and at Elizabeth City State University in North Carolina. Some poetry chapbooks include *Stashu Kapinski Strikes* Out (Rank Stranger Press), *Fatherhood at Fifty* (Tamafyhr Mountain Poetry), *Sketches of an Island Life* (dpi press), *Art Lessons* (Tamafyhr Mountain Poetry), *Letters to Wang Wei* (Pudding House Press), and *Stashu Kapinski Looks for Love* (erbacce-press, UK). After growing up under the shadow of Heppenstall Steel Mill in Pittsburgh, Pa., Joseph Lisowski has spent much of his life near the sea, including 10 years in the Caribbean, which serves as the setting for his three published mystery novels, *Full Body Rub, Looking For Lisa*, and *Looking For Lauren*. Joseph Lisowski won the University of North Carolina Board of Governors Teacher of the Year Award (2013-2014). His most recent poetry book publications are *Stashu Kapinski Dreams of Glory* (full length, Sweatshoppe Publications, 2013) and *Blue Season* (with Steve Klepetar, chapbook, mgv2>publishing, 2013).

KIRK MARSHALL

Kirk Marshall (@AttackRetweet) is a Brisbane-born writer and teacher living in Melbourne, Australia. He has written for more than eighty publications, both in Australia and overseas, including *Vol. 1 Brooklyn* (U.S.A.), *Word Riot* (U.S.A.), *3:AM Magazine* (France), *Le Zaporogue* (France/Denmark), *(Short) Fiction Collective* (U.S.A.), *The Vein* (U.S.A.), *Danse Macabre* (U.S.A.), *WHOLE BEAST RAG* (U.S.A.), *Gone Lawn* (U.S.A.), *The Seahorse Rodeo Folk Review* (U.S.A.), *The Journal of Unlikely Entomology* (U.S.A.) and *Kizuna: Fiction for Japan* (Japan). He edits *Red Leaves*, the English-language / Japanese bi-lingual literary journal. He now suffers migraines in two languages.

FRANCO STRONG

Franco Strong takes his inspiration in equal measure from his philosophical studies and the almost ceaseless sunshine of Southern California/Northern Mexico. His work centers on the US/Mexico border and the ethereal space it occupies both geographically and psychologically.

SARAH T.

Sarah T. is a poet and spoken word performer. Her first book, *This Past Was Waiting for Me*, is a collection of poetry and epistolary prose that explores the manner in which the past—especially America's colonial past and the race-class hierarchies that it established—plays out in the present. The excerpt of her novel-in-progress included in this volume evolved out of work she did as a creative writing fellow at Hambidge Center for the Arts in Rabun Gap, Georgia. Her other work has appeared in *Everyday Feminism*, *The Rumpus*, and *Sally Hemmings Dreams 'zine*. Sarah T. is also Sarah J. Trembath, a graduate of Temple and Howard universities and an American University writing instructor. She lives in Anacostia, SE, DC with her husband and son.

GUSTAVO ALBERTO GARCIA VACA

Gustavo Alberto Garcia Vaca is a multidisciplinary artist and writer. Gustavo's artworks have been exhibited in museums and art galleries including ICA in London; LACMA in Los Angeles; and Parco Museum, the Museum of Emerging Science and Innovation and the Mori Museum/Mado Lounge in Tokyo. His writing has been published in literary anthologies and journals including *Rattle* and *The Bilingual Review*. His artwork appears on T-shirts created by BEAMS T and SOPHNET. and on Be@rbrick toys released by Medicom Toy Corporation. Gustavo creates artwork for record covers, websites and live concert projections for musicians including the Foundation of Jazz artists Alice Coltrane and John Coltrane; Detroit Techno producer/DJ Jeff Mills; and Francois K's Deep Space dub record label. Gustavo's collaborative artwork with art director Hideki Nakajima was awarded by the Type Directors Club NYC, included in the *TYPOGRAPHY 30* art book published by Collins Design and exhibited at the Centre Pompidou in Paris. Gustavo's website is: http://www.chamanvision.com/

MONIKA MCGREAL VIOLA

Monika McGreal Viola is a writer based in Washington, DC. She holds a B.A. in Middle East Studies from Brown University, and master degrees in Fiction Writing from Johns Hopkins University and Anglo-Irish Writing from Trinity College, Dublin. Her fiction and poetry has appeared in Hermeneutic Chaos, Steel Toe Review, Icarus, and Thirteen Ways, among others. Find her at monikamcgrealviola.com.

SUSAN E. WADDS

Winner of The Writers' Union of Canada's 2016 short prose contest for developing writers, Susan E. Wadds' award-winning short fiction and poetry have been featured in various literary journals and anthologies, including *Room*, and carte blanche magazines. A graduate of the Humber School for Writers, Susan is certified in the Amherst Writers and Artists (AWA) method of writing workshop facilitation. She is Past President of the Writers' Community of Simcoe County (WCSC).

FERGUSON WILLIAMS

Ferguson Williams resides in and writes from Socastee, South Carolina. Her craftsmanship is a mixture of Kush, Cognac, and Cigarettes and as a result her debut novel will be titled such. A lover of English and Psychology, she is forever trying to find the right blend of the two in the hopes of leaving the reader wanting more. Always grinding, she can be reached at author.fwilliams@yahoo.com.

AZURE: A Journal of Literary Thought
www.LazuliLiteraryGroup.com

NOTES

www.ingramcontent.com/pod-product-compliance
Lightning Source LLC
Chambersburg PA
CBHW082102090726
47910CB00008B/2569

* 9 7 8 0 9 9 9 4 2 4 3 0 8 *